PLANTERS,
PIRATES,
& PATRIOTS

Other Books by Rod Gragg

Confederate Goliath: The Battle of Fort Fisher
The Illustrated Confederate Reader
The Old West Quiz and Fact Book
The Civil War Quiz and Fact Book
Bobby Bagley: POW

PLANTERS, PIRATES, & PATRIOTS

Historical Tales from the South Carolina Grand Strand

ROD GRAGG

Rutledge Hill Press
Nashville, Tennessee

To the memory of
William N. Outlaw, Jr.,
a genuine war hero
and a good man

Copyright © 1985, 1994 Rodney Oakley Gragg

Published in Nashville, Tennessee, by Rutledge Hill Press, Inc., 211 Seventh Avenue North, Nashville, Tennessee 37219.

Typography: D&T/Bailey Typesetting, Inc., Nashville, Tennessee

Library of Congress Cataloging-in-Publication Data

Gragg, Rod.
  [Pirates, planters & patriots]
  Planters, pirates & patriots : historical tales from the South
Carolina Grand Strand / Rod Gragg.
    p. cm.
  Originally published under title: Pirates, planters & patriots.
  Includes bibliographical references (p.) and index.
  ISBN 1-55853-293-5
  1. Myrtle Beach Region (S.C.) —History.   2. Horry County
(S.C.) —History.   3. Georgetown County (S.C.) —History.
  I. Title: Planters, pirates, and patriots.
  F279.M93G73 1994
  975.7'87—dc20   94–13994
                                                           CIP

Printed in the United States of America

1 2 3 4 5 6 7 8 — 99 98 97 96 95 94

CONTENTS

INTRODUCTION

FROM LITTLE RIVER TO GEORGETOWN THE
South Carolina Grand Strand is only fifty-five miles
long, yet few coastlines have a richer, more colorful
history. The Grand Strand was the home of Indians
and the haunt of pirates. It lured adventurers to
their doom. It created an empire of almost legendary wealth and power. It is the birthplace of
famous figures and the resting place of obscure
heroes. Numbered among its parade of colorful
characters are hardened explorers, seasoned
woodsmen, remarkable women, famous soldiers,
powerful politicians, men of violence, rich men,
poor men, and gifted visionaries.

Although the term "Grand Strand" is modern in
its origin, it is used throughout this book as the best
phrase to describe the coastal region of Horry and
Georgetown counties. Likewise, the familiar
"Charleston" is used for the famous port once
known as "Charles Town," and "Conway" replaces
the older "Conwayboro."

Historians are still debating the exact site of the
Spanish colony of San Miguel de Gualdape. Some
scholars are certain it lay somewhere outside of the

Grand Strand. Others are positive it was situated on Winyah Bay, which is where this book places it.

This work is not a chronological survey, although the stories are loosely arranged in chronological order. Neither is this book meant to be a formal history of the Grand Strand, although history has not been sacrificed for romance anywhere in this narrative.

The history of the South Carolina Grand Strand has more than enough color without invention. The true stories within this book are proof of that.

CHAPTER ONE

THE
LOST COLONY
OF SAN MIGUEL

HE LEANED ON THE SHIP'S RAILING AND stared across the gray Atlantic at the distant coastline. For six years he had dreamed of this moment. He had plotted, lobbied, argued, and invested a fortune to stand where he now stood—on the deck of his flagship looking at the forested shores of the mysterious New World. If successful, he would make history as the man who established the first Spanish colony on the mainland of North America.

His name was Lucas Vásquez de Ayllón, and he came to the American coast in 1526, more than a century before the region was colonized by the English. Sailing with his flagship were five other

Spanish caravels. Aboard them were five hundred Spanish settlers from the Caribbean colony of Hispaniola, an uncounted number of slaves, and three Dominican friars.

Historians still debate the site where de Ayllón established his North American colony, but some are certain the spot lay on the banks of Winyah Bay on the southern end of the modern Grand Strand. If so, the hazy, bumpy coastline de Ayllón stared at this July day in 1526, the place his ships made land-fall, would one day be known as North Carolina's Cape Fear region. Just out of sight to the southwest stretched the wooded shore that would become the South Carolina Grand Strand. De Ayllón called his new colony San Miguel de Gualdape—the colony of Saint Michael—and he hoped it would establish Spain's claim to the uncharted northern continent before the despised French and English could settle the vast land and harvest its riches.

De Ayllón's plans for his colony began six years earlier, in 1520, when he dispatched an expedition to the mysterious mainland. Intelligent and well-educated, with high-ranking friends, he had gone to Hispaniola from Spain years before to serve as auditor of the colony. He was given an initial salary of four hundred Indian slaves, which he converted into a personal fortune. However, unlike many Spanish conquistadors of his day, de Ayllón was reputed to be a man of principle, relatively devoid of the brutality attributed to many explorers of the New World.

As a royal official in the gateway colony of Hispaniola, he was constantly exposed to schemes

Lucas Vasquez de Ayllón fit this image of the Spanish nobleman of his day.

for reaping the riches of the New World, and eventually, he became enchanted with the idea of finding wealth and glory on the unknown North American continent. He received the Spanish king's permission to finance an exploratory voyage to the continent, and in 1520 he dispatched a seasoned sea captain named Francisco Gordillo on an expedition to find a site for a colony.

Gordillo at first turned the exploratory voyage into a search for slaves. After several months of searching fruitlessly for Indian captives in the Caribbean, Gordillo's caravel was joined by another Spanish ship and the two captains decided to explore the mainland, where they might find their human prey. In June 1521 they reached what is believed to be today's Carolina's coast, where a storm drove them into the mouth of a large river. The next day when the gale subsided, they surveyed the water they had been blown into and named it Rio de San Juan Bautista—the River of Saint John the Baptist.

When the two ships probed upriver, a group of Indians appeared on shore, cautiously studying the peculiar ships until Gordillo sent a landing party of bearded Spaniards toward shore in small boats. The

Indians fled in terror, but the landing party somehow captured two of them, dressed them in Spanish clothing, and returned them to their village. Reassured by this treatment, the tribal chieftain sent a delegation of Indians to the Spaniards with presents of food.

With friendly relations established, Gordillo went ashore with some of his sailors on 30 June 1521 and carved crosses into several large trees, officially claiming the region for Spain's King Charles V. Later the Spaniards explored inland and received gifts of furs, pearls, and silver from the Indians. The Spanish captains agreed that the land was rich and fertile and seemed ideal for the colony de Ayllón wanted to establish.

After gaining the trust of the natives, the Spaniards invited 150 unsuspecting Indians aboard the two ships, guided them into the holds, then quietly raised anchor and sailed for Hispaniola with the Indians as slaves. One ship was lost on the voyage, and although the surviving Indians were later freed in Hispaniola, most of them starved themselves to death grieving for home.

De Ayllón was excited by the glowing reports of good land and potential riches and especially by the remarkable tales recounted by a resourceful Indian survivor who learned to speak Spanish. Called Francisco Chicora by the Spaniards, he told amazing stories of his homeland, where, he said, treasure abounded and a giant king and queen ruled over a bizarre race of men with long inflexible tails. De Ayllón accepted the fantastic stories about Chicora's land—even when the innovative Indian explained that the people with tails had to cut holes in their chairs in order to sit.

Motivated by the prospect of adventure, honor, and wealth, de Ayllón petitioned King Charles for permission to establish a colony in the land of Chicora. The king made de Ayllón the governor of Chicora and gave him permission to establish a colony at his own expense, provided the profits from newly discovered gold and silver would go to the king and provided that de Ayllón would build a church and monastery in Chicora.

De Ayllón readily agreed to the king's terms and recruited colonists for his expedition. The Spanish citizens of Hispaniola were eager to seek their fortunes among the riches of Chicora. Five hundred of them signed up as colonists, depleting the European population of Hispaniola to such an extent that officials in Spain worried about the expedition's impact on Spain's flagship colony. De Ayllón assembled a fleet of six caravels and a tender, stocked a large supply of provisions, and armed his ships with artillery from Spain.

After a series of frustrating delays, the fleet finally raised sail and left Hispaniola for the new colony in Chicora. Aboard de Ayllón's ships were the five hundred colonists, the friars, the slaves, a unit of soldiers, an official treasurer, a government accountant, an agent of the king, eighty-nine horses, and a group of Indian interpreters who were the survivors of Gordillo's expedition. Among the interpreters was Francisco Chicora, who may have invented his stories of riches and wonders simply to engineer a ride home.

De Ayllón's colonists at first established friendly relations
with Native Americans.

Although he remained safely behind on
Hispaniola during Gordillo's preparatory explo-
ration, de Ayllón chose to lead the 1526 expedition
and to serve on the site as governor of the new
colony. After days on the open sea, the lookouts
finally sighted land at the entrance to a large river.
Was it the Cape Fear River near modern-day Wilmington, North Carolina?

De Ayllón ordered the fleet to enter the river and
undoubtedly watched with mounting excitement
from the deck. As the ships neared land, however,
the expedition encountered its first disaster: One of
the ships struck a shoal and tore open its hull.
Everyone aboard was rescued, but the ship went
down with all its valuable provisions.

De Ayllón put ashore a landing party led by Francisco Chicora and the Indian interpreters and received another setback: As soon as the Indians entered the forest, they ran away. Chicora must have laughed aloud as he ran through the forest, elated that his tales of glory had brought him back to the continent after five years with the Spaniards. Not only did the grim-faced members of the landing party have to report the loss of the Indian interpreters, but they also found no sign of the site Gordillo had discovered in 1521. If de Ayllón wanted to find Chicora's land he would have to look elsewhere and do so without Francisco Chicora.

De Ayllón decided to move on and set his sailors to work constructing a new vessel for the passengers of the sunken caravel. In remarkable time the Spanish seamen constructed a small, single-masted ship with oars and a sail—the first European ship built on the North American continent—and the colonists were ready to continue their search for a site to settle.

While the ship was under construction, de Ayllón sent a coasting party to examine the area and was rewarded with a positive report: To the southwest of the expedition's landfall lay a long, smooth beach. If de Ayllón had come ashore at the mouth of the Cape Fear River, the area to the southwest could only have been the region that would someday be known as the South Carolina Grand Strand.

Leaving the women and the weak aboard ship, the male colonists walked southwestward along shore, followed by the ships, which provided crossings at inlets along the way. The expedition followed the coastline for days until de Ayllón and his colonists stood at the edge of what some historians are certain was Winyah Bay, the wide freshwater bay at the south end of today's Grand Strand. There they stopped.

They studied the terrain around them—a picturesque, unspoiled land of forests and marshes surrounding a sparkling bay. It had all the ingredients for a successful colony: good soil, high ground close to an ample supply of fresh water, easy access to the ocean, and abundant game. Looking at a region unrivaled in natural beauty, de Ayllón made his decision: He would establish his colony on the edge of this great bay. He declared this to be the site of San Miguel de Gualdape, which, he hoped, would become the capital of Spanish North America.

The once quiet woodlands overlooking the bay soon echoed the chop of axes and the babble of excited voices as the crude wilderness settlement of San Miguel emerged from the forest. Spanish scouting parties discovered Indian villages nearby, where natives dwelt in huts roofed with pine branches. Armed with bows of chestnut, the Indians displayed remarkable skill as archers and appeared formidable if forced into combat with the colonists. Under de Ayllón's direction, however, friendly relations were established with the neighboring Indians, and the Spanish settlement was constructed with no threat of attack.

De Ayllón's hopes for his colony soon were confronted with a disappointing truth: If he had found the land of Chicora, it did not match the glorious

De Ayllón's colonists hoped to expand the Spanish Empire into North America. *(From the original painting, "The First Tanner," by Mort Künstler. Copyright 1972 Mort Künstler, Inc.)*

descriptions promoted by Francisco Chicora. De Ayllón saw no sign of gold or silver around Winyah Bay. Nor did he find long-tailed natives, giant rulers, or a rich civilization. All he found in the Indian camps were smoke-filled bark huts, gardens of squash and corn, and a primitive people engaged in the daily routines of survival. It was a beautiful and fertile land, but it was not the rich Chicora envisioned by de Ayllón and his colonists.

De Ayllón still held great hopes for his colony, but they were short-lived. Even while San Miguel was under construction, everything began to go wrong. The malaria season was at its peak, promoted by legions of mosquitoes. Although they did not know why, the settlers began to sicken. First they became weak, then they were stricken by fever. The fever rose until they were bedridden.

Finally, if it continued, they became delirious and died. Almost every family was stricken, and hastily dug graves multiplied daily.

The epidemic left few men to clear timber, build cabins, or prepare land for crops. The growing season passed quickly, and the provisions that had been lost in the shipwreck could not be replaced. Winter came early in 1526 and was unusually severe. The freezing temperatures killed the mosquitoes and ended the fever but produced a wave of winter illnesses encouraged by the colonists' poor diet. Soon the food from Hispaniola was gone, and the settlers were forced to depend on fish from the bay. As more people died, fewer men were healthy enough to catch all the fish needed to feed the colony. By late October those laid in the shallow graves included victims of starvation.

San Miguel was dying, and de Ayllón could do nothing to stop it. In October he too became ill. On 18 October 1526 he died. His dreams of riches and glory as the founder of Spain's northern empire died with him.

Command of San Miguel fell to de Ayllón's chief aide, Francisco Gómez, but rebellion began with de Ayllón's death. Instead of gold and silver and the fabulous treasures of Chicora, the colonists had found nothing but hardship and death—and some of them were angry. Two of the colony's soldiers organized a band of disgruntled settlers who captured Gómez and his aides. The leaders of the mutiny then declared themselves in power, imposed strict military law over the colony, and instead of seeking help from the natives, attacked them.

The colonists soon wished they could restore Gómez to power again, and some slaves took the initiative by burning the cabin of one of the mutiny leaders. The settlers who were strong enough to fight managed to capture the rebel leaders and released Gómez and his men. The mutiny's main leader was executed, and the other rebel leaders were imprisoned. By the time Gómez regained control, however, conditions in San Miguel looked hopeless. De Ayllón and his vision were gone. Only 150 of the original 500 colonists were still alive. The colony had been shaken by the mutiny, and the surviving slaves seemed likely to revolt. The Indians had been antagonized and were now hostile. No crops existed, and those settlers who survived the winter would have to endure another season of fever.

Gómez and his advisers decided to abandon San Miguel. The surviving Spanish colonists walked away from their crude log homes and boarded their ships to return to Hispaniola. Even on the return voyage, the would-be colonists were struck by tragedy. A winter gale caught the tiny flotilla on the open sea. Seven passengers froze to death during the storm, and the tender, which was carrying de Ayllón's body, was sunk.

De Ayllón's wife and son had remained in Hispaniola, waiting to join him when the colony was established. Instead, they were left in grief. As heirs of the failed colony of San Miguel, they eventually received an extension of the colony's charter from the king, but they were unable to interest anyone in a renewed attempt at colonization. Years later they died in poverty.

More than five hundred Spanish colonists tried—and failed—
to establish the capital of Spanish North America on a site
some historians believe to have been the Grand Strand's
Winyah Bay.

The Spanish were never able to establish a secure
colony north of Florida, and, as they feared, the
North American continent was eventually settled
by the French and English. Had de Ayllón's colony
proved successful, however, America might have
been established not by the English at Jamestown,
Virginia, in 1607, but by Lucas Vásquez de Ayllón
in 1526 at San Miguel in Spanish North America.

CHAPTER TWO

"A

VERY WILD AND

SAVAGE PEOPLE"

WHEN WILLIAM WAITES LOOKED AT HIS NEW trading post, he didn't see much. It was a small log hut with a dirt floor, but with it Waites planned to make his fortune. A native of Wales in the British Isles, he was one of South Carolina's colonial factors—an official trader granted a government license to trade with the Indians.

In 1716 he brought carpenters from faraway Charleston to build the tiny cabin. It stood on a slight bluff overlooking the dark, slow-moving Black River, not far from Winyah Bay. Waites could see up and down the river for a long distance, but on the land side of his trading post he was surrounded by a seemingly endless forest. Back in Charleston and in distant London they called the forest the "Howling Wilderness." Perhaps the name came from the wolves or the wind, or perhaps from the isolation of the great forest, which eventually made a man want to howl—either from the pain of loneliness or from the fear that sometimes seemed to creep out of the woods at dark.

The forest started right at the ocean, and it kept on going as far west as anybody had ever been. It wasn't like the forests of Europe, where the woods were broken by roads and fields and villages. This was America and the forest seemed endless. You could follow an animal path or an Indian trail through it, and you might come to an Indian village with a cornfield behind it. But the great forest surrounded everything, and no one Waites knew had ever seen the end of it.

That's why you traveled by river in the colonies, and that's why he built his trading post on the river near Winyah Bay. The furs he got from the Indians and the trade goods he gave them could move along the river faster than anyone could move overland. The trade goods came upriver from Charleston, and the furs went downriver to the city. Furs brought a good price in England. That's why the colonial government wanted to stimulate a brisker trade with the Winyahs and the Waccamaws.

In exchange for coats, shirts, English blankets, beads from Italy, forged knives, flintlocks, and rum, the Waccamaws, Winyahs, and other natives would trade furs: otter, mink, raccoon, an occasional wolf pelt, and deerskins—lots of deerskins. The tawny deer pelts were the staple of South Carolina's flourishing fur trade.

To get them you had to deal with the Indians. Waites trusted the Winyahs, but he had been warned about the Waccamaws. The English detested dealing with the Waccamaws, one of the largest tribes in the eastern part of the colony, but standing on the river bluff in front of his new trading post, Waites knew they would soon come. One morning he would see them paddling up the river in their peculiar dugout canoes, or one afternoon, just before dusk, they would quietly appear from the forest. What the trader didn't know was that the fur trade on Winyah Bay would have a short life. So would the Waccamaws. In less than a decade they would be gone.

No one knows when they first appeared. Sometime, perhaps before Columbus, they followed the coast or the rivers into the dense woods and wild swamps that once surrounded the Grand Strand. They were not the first Indians to live there. Others came before them, but they left or were forced out by the Waccamaws.

In the early eighteenth century, a few decades after the English had established a settlement near the site of Charleston, curious colonists exploring the northern coast found the Waccamaws living in villages east of the Pee Dee River. "Waccamaw" was what they called themselves, or at least that's how the name sounded to the Englishmen, who applied it to the main waterway of the region.

Distantly related to the warlike Sioux of the Great Plains, the Waccamaws were seminomadic river

Indians who were isolated in one of the densest regions of the great American wilderness, occupying a harsh, swampy land that was almost impossible to penetrate. In their remote, hostile homeland, surrounded by waterways, they lived with little fear of attack by enemies. Such isolation made them among the last of the coastal tribes to have contact with the English colonists.

The Englishmen came to South Carolina in 1670 and established a colony near modern Charleston. Not until 1716, when Waites established his trading post, did English colonists develop contacts with the remote Waccamaws. In exchange for fur pelts, the Waccamaws received English goods and occasionally some cattle for butchering. They quickly developed a taste for beef and were accused of stealing cattle from the pastures cleared by the first Englishmen who settled near Winyah Bay.

The Waccamaws may have been intrigued with English goods and food, but the establishment of William Waites's trading post began the decline of the tribe. In their smoky, bark huts, the Waccamaw women prepared meals of venison, shad, and mullet flavored by hickory nuts, acorns, and roots. Other delicacies were boiled goose, barbecued raccoon, and a baked breadlike dish. The men of the tribe, living and traveling along the Waccamaw River, hacked swift, sturdy dugout canoes from fallen cypress trees. Speeding up and down the waterways, they fished and transported their furs to the trading posts. They provided a dependable diet of freshwater fish by weaving large nets from reeds. To capture venison for the pot, they fired the

The Waccamaws used speedy dugout canoes to travel the area's waterways.

canebrakes where the deer hid by day, driving the deer into the open where they could be killed by bow and arrow.

The Waccamaws were part of a loose confederation of approximately twenty tribes, including the Santees, the Sampits, and the Winyahs—who lived near Winyah Bay—and the Pee Dees, Cheraws, and Catawbas, who lived farther inland.

The English colonists found nothing noble about the Waccamaws. Early explorers who dealt with the tribes described them as primitive and decadent. British officials called them "a very wild and savage people," who were perhaps the most "barbarous" tribe in the colony. What the Waccamaws thought of the English, who enslaved thousands of Indians, was never recorded.

Life for South Carolina's Indians held additional hazards after the British established their colony. The Lords Proprietors, who administered the colony, granted the colonists permission to enslave all hostile Indians and sell them in the Caribbean slave trade. The potential profits encouraged the colonists to promote both warfare and slave trading, making South Carolina the leading exporter of Indian slaves among the English colonies in North America.

The Seewees, a tribe living near Winyah Bay, fell victim to the slave trade en masse. Noting that the colonists to whom they sold furs loaded the pelts onto ships for resale in England, the Seewees decided to eliminate the middle man. They reasoned that they could make a greater profit if they took the furs directly to England. So they amassed a

Indians like the Waccamaws made deerskins a valuable colonial period export.

great collection of furs, loaded the entire tribe into a fleet of canoes, and set out across the Atlantic Ocean. At sea a storm swamped many of their canoes, and the surviving Seewees were "rescued" by a passing English merchant vessel. When the ship docked in the Caribbean, the Seewees were sold into slavery, leaving their nation as nothing but a footnote in history.

Not all Europeans looked upon the Native Americans of the Carolinas as mere warriors or trading partners. Some genuinely tried to understand their ways and learn worthwhile skills from Indians like the Waccamaws. A hardy, compassionate handful of colonists endured severe hardship even to the point of death in order to carry the gospel of Jesus Christ to these first Americans. In the William Clark Doub papers at Duke University's Perkins Library is a remarkable collection of documents from Peter and Michael Doub, two itinerant Methodist ministers who carried the Word to the Carolina backwoods almost two hundred years ago. Among those whose eternal lives they sought to save and enrich were Native Americans, and their records include a poignant partial testimony by an Indian woman happily converted to Christianity, yet temporarily struggling with her cultural identity.

"When me was first converted," she reported, "me love Christians and Christian ministers as me love me own soul; but me grow vile, very big and me no love Christian ministers. Me was one day in swamp cutting broom stick, when the Spirit said to me, 'Indian why you no love Christians or Christian ministers?' Me say, 'Because me know more than all of them.' The Spirit tell me, 'Indian you lost your humble.' And when me look for me humble, me humble was gone. Then me go back."

Although colonial law forbade the enslavement of friendly tribes, the Indians living around Winyah Bay steadily declined in numbers during the first half-century of British colonization. The Sampits disappeared without a record. The Santees, who were left with less than fifty warriors by 1717, fought an ill-fated skirmish with the colonists and disappeared into Caribbean slavery. The Winyahs managed to postpone their demise by serving as mercenaries for the colonists in wars against other tribes. The Waccamaws, isolated in the wilderness along the Waccamaw River, retained tribal strength into the second decade of the eighteenth century.

A 1715 British census of South Carolina's Indians listed the Waccamaws as the largest coastal tribe north of Charleston. Six Waccamaw villages were counted by the census takers, who placed the Waccamaw population at 610 men, women, and children. Five years later, however, a confrontation between the Waccamaws and the colonists destroyed the tribe.

Today no one knows what caused the brief Waccamaw War, but relations between the Waccamaws and the colonists had deteriorated by 1720. For years the colonists had blamed the Waccamaws for the disappearance of English cattle. After the Yamassee War in 1715, in which scores of Englishmen living west of Charleston had been massacred, concern about the Waccamaws began to build among the colonists in the Winyah Bay area. In 1717, shortly after William Waites opened his trading post on the Black River, the Waccamaws moved from their villages on Waccamaw Neck and along the Waccamaw River to new sites on the south side of the Black River, near Winyah Bay. The reason for the move is unclear, but it worried the nervous settlers living up the Black River. The Cheraws lived north of them, and the colonists were afraid of being trapped between the two tribes.

The Waccamaws declared good intentions, and some of their leaders even ventured to Charleston to consult with British officials. But the colonists remained suspicious. Colonial leaders urged the Waccamaws to return to their old village sites, but the Waccamaws refused. When the colonial government outlawed trade with the Waccamaws as punishment for their refusal, the Waccamaws established a black market with illegal traders anxious to acquire their valuable furs.

Relations between the Waccamaws and the colonists continued to worsen, and finally, in 1720, the dispute exploded into a brief, violent conflict. The only official report of the fighting is a solitary British reference to "a small war with the Vocamas." Nothing exists to reveal which side began the bloodshed, but it ended in disaster for the Indians. Armed English colonists supported by Winyah mercenaries attacked the Waccamaws, who could muster no more than one hundred warriors. When the fighting ended, at least sixty Waccamaws were dead or enslaved.

Like many tribes of their day, the Waccamaws had a formidable reputation.

The surviving members of the tribe may have fled inland to join the distant Catawbas or tribes in North Carolina. A decade later, in 1730, a handful of Waccamaws still lived along the Waccamaw River, but that year the British records made their final reference to the tribe. Those who survived slavery and the 1720 war may have succumbed to disease or alcoholism, or they may have melted into other tribes to the west.

A few years after it opened, William Waites's trading post on the Black River stood vacant and abandoned. It was no longer needed: The Indians were gone.

CHAPTER THREE

THE WILD, WILD WEST OF THE EAST

IN THE RIVERFRONT VILLAGE OF KINGSTON, Joseph Jerdon was known as a man to avoid. He had a quick temper, he drank too much, and sometimes when he strode down the settlement's dirt streets he carried a sword. Tough characters were not unusual in Kingston in 1767. The village was barely thirty years old, but it already had a reputation in colonial South Carolina as the rough, brawling little port on the Waccamaw River.

Another townsman with a mean reputation was tavern owner John McDugall, who was the village justice of the peace when not selling the strong, eyewatering ale frontiersmen called punch. Within a generation colonial Kingston would become the town of Conwayboro, which would later be known as Conway—the seat of Horry County and the gateway to the Grand Strand. The town had a hard beginning, and the rugged characters who stalked its streets and loitered on its docks gave it an image of independence and defiance that would last for generations.

That image went on record one mild day in 1767 when Joseph Jerdon and John McDugall came to blows. The argument began with an idle remark that passed between the two as Jerdon guzzled ale in McDugall's tavern. The comment has been lost to history, but it caused Jerdon's hair-trigger temper to flare. He waved his sword menacingly in McDugall's face.

Apparently accustomed to such frontier displays of bravado in his tavern, McDugall tried to laugh away the threat. "It's a pity to take away a man's life with such a rusty weapon as that," he joked, pointing to Jerdon's drawn blade.

In response Jerdon unleashed a string of oaths, insulting the tavern keeper's Scottish background and accusing him of harboring canine ancestry. Angered, McDugall defiantly closed his bar and ordered Jerdon to pay his hefty, overdue bar bill.

"You keep a tavern and won't serve me punch?" Jerdon yelled. "You Scotch scoundrel! I'll post you as a coward in Georgetown!"

Stomping outside, Jerdon began pacing up and down the street, shouting that McDugall was a coward who hid behind his wife's skirts. Furious at the accusations, McDugall stormed out of his tavern and confronted Jerdon in the street. Undeterred, Jerdon threatened to send a slave for ale from Mrs. Wilson's tavern, McDugall's competition.

"If you bring punch in here," McDugall warned, "I'll break the bowl in your face!"

"Will you?" Jerdon retorted.

"I will!" McDugall shouted.

"Advance!" Jerdon yelled and placed the point of his sword on the tavern keeper's chest. From a pocket, McDugall produced a large knife, and the two men squared off in the dirt street. Residents of the village began running toward the fight, and deckhands on the schooners docked nearby at the town wharf stopped their work to watch.

The rough little settlement of Kingston perched on a bluff overlooking a bend in the Waccamaw River about fifteen miles inland from the Atlantic. It had been cut out of the forest in the 1730s as part of the township scheme developed by Robert Johnson, one of the early royal governors of South Carolina.

When Johnson took office in Charleston in 1730, he was worried. Almost all of the fledgling colony's thin population was centered in Charleston, where the colony had begun sixty years earlier in 1670. Johnson was afraid such concentration made the colony vulnerable to a Spanish invasion, an Indian uprising, or a slave revolt. What the colony needed, he believed, was to increase its population and disperse the colonists farther inland, making the colony a less tempting target.

The governor submitted a plan to the colonial legislature that called for creation of eleven new river settlements sixty to one hundred miles inland from Charleston. Each settlement would consist of a town and a surrounding township. The plan included two townships on the Altamaha River, two on the Savannah, two on the Santee, and one each on the Wateree, the Pon Pon, the Black, the Pee Dee, and the Waccamaw. The two townships on the Altamaha fell into the new colony of Georgia, but the others were organized as planned.

The new township on the wild Waccamaw was surveyed, and a site was selected. The center of the township lay on high ground over a picturesque creek of the Waccamaw, which was deemed "much the boldest river in South Carolina" by the men who paddled upriver to examine the township site.

The Waccamaw River township was named Kingston in honor of King George II, who ruled the worldwide British Empire at the time. New immigrants to the colony were promised a string of inducements if they chose to settle in Kingston or the other townships. The colonial government would give each new settler free transportation from Charleston to the township site, where he would be awarded fifty acres of free land for himself and each member of his household, including slaves. He would also receive free tools and enough free provisions to get a start toward taming the frontier.

On 26 February 1733 the South Carolina Upper House of Assembly and the royal governor, Robert Johnson, signed a resolution officially opening Kingston Township for settlement. The township covered much of what is now Horry County, and the town of Kingston lay on the site of what is now

The Kingston settlers hacked their home sites out of the dense forests along the Waccamaw River.

downtown Conway. However, settlers did not rush to Kingston, despite the inducements of the government. Perhaps the reputation of the Waccamaw wilderness discouraged settlement, or perhaps it simply took several years for the governor's plan to become known in Great Britain. Not until the late 1730s, almost five years after Kingston Township was devised, did settlers begin to come to the region with any regularity.

The first serious wave of settlers seems to have come to the township in 1737. They were Scotch-Irish Presbyterians looking for greater fortune and freedom in America. They arrived in Charleston after a grueling voyage of several months, in which they suffered misfortunes ranging from seasickness to scurvy. From Charleston they were ferried up the coast to the new, struggling port of Georgetown, where they were issued provisions and tools and the authority to claim land in the township of their choice. They apparently chose Kingston as their home, for in a few years an itinerant Presbyterian minister was making calls on a tiny congregation at Kingston on the Waccamaw.

These new settlers were dubbed "poor Protestants from Ireland" by the other British colonists. Like thousands of other immigrants to America, the Kingston settlers left Europe's good roads, pleasant fields, and neat stone fences to come to a new life on the South Carolina frontier. On the Waccamaw River they encountered a dense and swampy forest populated by bear, deer, and wolves and filled with bloodsucking insects by day and a multitude of strange noises by night.

They had to clear the forest, build log huts, pull up endless stumps or plow around them, and brave the rigors of frontier life far removed from the comforts and assistance of civilization. Living deep in the Howling Wilderness, they faced illness, isolation, deprivation, and loneliness. For many the ordeal began before they even reached the township. Some died of disease aboard ship. Others arrived in Charleston to find the promised transportation and provisions were unavailable because the government's township funds had disappeared.

In 1737 one group of Scotch-Irish immigrants who came to settle in South Carolina found the colony's legislature in a hot debate about the disappearance of the money. While the legislators loudly accused the governor of pilfering the funds, the newly arrived immigrants begged for food door to door in Charleston until the legislature made a new appropriation to send them inland.

When they finally arrived in Kingston, the first settlers found that the best farmland in the township had been taken by wealthy speculators who had no intentions of actually settling on their property, but planned to sell it for large profits. The immigrants were left with land too poor or swampy to produce ample crops. Faced with the possible failure of Kingston Township, the legislators called for an investigation to reveal the greedy land speculators who had endangered the township plan. Most of the speculators, the investigation revealed, were members of the legislature.

Settlement of Kingston was so slow that the legislature eventually declared the township to be a failure. Yet a trickle of settlers continued to come to the area, and those who adapted to the rigors of life on the Waccamaw stubbornly refused to leave. Slowly the crude settlement grew, and by the dawn of the American Revolution, Kingston and the surrounding township were firmly established. The people who chose to live on the rugged, isolated Waccamaw were a hardy stock who came to feel self-sufficient and independent of the rest of the colony.

It was in this frontier atmosphere that Joseph Jerdon and John McDugall faced each other on the street in Kingston that day in 1767. Jerdon quickly got the drop on McDugall. Placing the point of his sword on the tavern keeper's chest, Jerdon marched him backward, off the street and into a courtyard behind the tavern. Unable to reach Jerdon with his knife, McDugall backed across the courtyard, worked his way down some stairs, and backed across a plaza until he fell backward over a chair. Jerdon bent over McDugall with upraised sword, but McDugall quickly plunged his knife into Jerdon's stomach.

Mortally wounded, Jerdon dropped his sword, grabbed his stomach, and ran out into the street. "Stop the murderer!" he yelled. "I am a dead man!" McDugall chased his wounded adversary, and near the Kingston blacksmith's shop the two men scuffled briefly. Despite his wound, Jerdon struck McDugall over the head with a large barrel stave, leaving him momentarily stunned. Jerdon ran down the street several more yards, then collapsed and died. Onlookers who had watched the fight ran to the fallen man, but they were unable to help. McDugall, bruised but still antagonistic, pushed his way through the crowd and stood over the body.

"Better he lay there than me," he said, and cursed his fallen foe.

After the American Revolution, a measure of law and order came to Kingston, which also took on a new name. After the Revolution few people wanted to live in a place named for the king of England, so in 1801 Kingston was renamed Conway in honor of a South Carolina Revolutionary War officer, Robert Conway, who lived for a while in the town. The surrounding area was renamed Horry County for Peter Horry, a Waccamaw region planter who served prominently as an officer in the Revolution.

Like their colonial ancestors, generations of
Horry County residents were hardy, self-reliant,
and independent.
(Horry County Museum CNB Collection)

Despite the changes, the region's tough, independent reputation persisted. Northern visitors passing through Conway in the years before the Civil War risked mob punishment if found carrying abolitionist literature or even a copy of the *New York Tribune*. An English maid who visited the town in the second half of the nineteenth century was horrified by the number of dogs she encountered inside a Conway church during services and noted with dismay the number of tobacco-chewing worshipers who happily spat on the church floor.

Perhaps because of its colorful, spirited history, Horry County eventually became known as the Independent Republic of Horry. It was said that some residents of the county were so independent-minded in the nineteenth century that they used river turtles for money and little turtles for change.

Following World War II, however, tobacco, timber, and tourism made Horry County and its Grand Strand into one of the most progressive regions on the southern coast. Yet even as the region began attracting visitors by the millions, old-timers could still remember the days when Horry County was known as the Wild, Wild West of the East.

CHAPTER • FOUR

TERROR

OF THE

BLACK FLAG

IT'S THE BLACK FLAG!" YELLED THE LOOK-out from atop the ship's mainmast. Passengers and crewmen aboard the merchant vessel peered anxiously toward the distant ship on the horizon and felt fear rising within them. Above the mainsail of the ship bearing down on them fluttered a black banner adorned with a grisly skull and crossbones: the flag of death flown by the Carolina pirates.

Aboard the approaching ship were bearded, sunburned seamen armed with cutlasses and pistols. If they overtook the merchant ship, they would do what they wanted and no one could stop them. If satisfied with their booty, they might set the passengers and crew adrift in lifeboats and then sail away with the captured ship. If their mood was dark, however, they might casually murder everyone aboard. The passengers and crew of the merchant ship could only hope the wind would hold in their favor and that they could outdistance the pirates. Such encounters were common along America's eastern coastline in the colonial era.

In the early eighteenth century, as many as two thousand pirates operated off the coast of North America, and one of their major targets was Charleston, the busiest, most important port in the southern colonies.

Piracy in North America began soon after the discovery of the New World. Spain and England warred with each other for control of the newly discovered wealth of the Americas and as part of the constant wars that plagued Europe during the colonization of the New World. Both sides outfitted pirate ships to raid enemy shipping, vainly seeking to disguise their actions by calling the marauding seamen "privateers." Regardless of name, they behaved like pirates, capturing and looting both armed and unarmed enemy ships. The coastal waters off the Spanish mainland colonies of South America, the Spanish Main, became a nest of piracy.

When Spain and England ceased fighting, many of the privateers dropped the pretense and began raiding ships of their native countries as well as those of the former enemy. The English West Indies became a pirate stronghold and so did the Caribbean islands of the Bahamas, Jamaica, and Tortuga. By 1700 pirates were capturing British

Pirates like this grim sea hawk preyed on ships in the sea-lanes off the Grand Strand in the eighteenth century.

ships with a frequency that threatened English commerce in North America. Finally, in 1717 King George I offered amnesty to all who would cease piracy and take a royal pardon. Some pirates accepted the offer, but others chose to battle tighter policing by the British navy. Most simply left the Caribbean and sailed for the North American mainland, where they resumed their raids with fewer risks.

The unpopular trade laws imposed on the American colonies by the British Parliament severely hiked the price of imported goods and encouraged demand for lower-priced, pirated goods in the American colonies. In seaports from Charleston to Boston merchants put aside ethics, asked few questions, and bought the cheaper goods sold on the pirate black markets.

Some colonies indirectly encouraged piracy, and South Carolina was one of the worst offenders. During the early eighteenth century South Carolina's colonial government allowed pirate black markets to flourish in Charleston despite the objections of officials back in London. At least one member of the colony's legislature was banished from office for dealing with pirates, and a royal governor, John Archdale, was accused of using his office to protect them. Defended by sympathetic officials, infamous pirates docked their ships in Charleston and brazenly strolled the city's brick streets, unafraid of prosecution. Eventually, less-permissive members of the colony's legislature enacted laws restricting piracy, and the swaggering seahawks disappeared from Charleston's streets.

A 1742 view of Charleston from the harbor.

They did not leave South Carolina waters, however. The Carolina pirates who raided shipping in the sea-lanes off the Grand Strand favored small, fast vessels that could easily overtake a large quarry, then escape into the coastal shallows, where heavy warships could not follow. The shallow creeks and inlets along the Grand Strand made ideal haunts for the Carolina pirates. In secluded places like Little River and Murrells Inlet, they could careen their ships—tilt them to one side in the shallows—and scrape off the barnacles that reduced a ship's speed. Freshly scraped and resupplied with drinking water, pirate vessels would leave the inlets and prowl the waters off the Grand Strand, searching for merchant ships ferrying goods between the northern and southern colonies.

When a ship fell into pirate hands, all valuables would be removed, and everyone aboard, if lucky, would be set adrift in boats or marooned on shore while the pirates sailed away with the plundered ship in tow. Merchant ships could sometimes escape if the wind was in their sails or if they could muster enough gunfire. Pirates seldom liked a brisk fight, so they tortured and murdered seamen who resisted, as examples to others. Often merchant crews promptly surrendered their ships when overtaken, unwilling to die and hopeful that the pirates would be satisfied with booty instead of blood.

The pirates who lurked off the Carolina coast were a bizarre lot:

• Capt. **William Fly,** a former boxer from Jamaica, led a mutiny in 1726, murdered the officers of his ship, and took command. His pirate career lasted only a month, but he managed to plunder several ships off the Carolina coast before he sailed for New England, where he was caught and executed.

• Capt. **George Lowther** was another mutineer. He enjoyed a long career as a pirate, but his life also ended in violence. After assembling a pirate fleet and harassing shipping up and down the North American coast, he was badly beaten in a naval battle off South Carolina when his ship ran aground. He waded ashore, disappeared into the Carolina forest, and later committed suicide.

• **Christopher Moody** may have been the youngest pirate roaming Grand Strand waters. He was twenty-three when he became a pirate captain. After plundering ships off South Carolina, he

Passengers and crewmen captured by pirates often suffered a grisly fate.

shifted operations to West Africa, where he was eventually captured and hanged.

• **Anne Bonney,** an infamous female pirate, was the daughter of a prominent Carolina planter. As a young woman, she ran away with a sailor and became a pirate in the Caribbean. Bonney was known for her ruthlessness and repeatedly raided the South Carolina coast until captured. She was found guilty of piracy, but if she was hanged it was done secretly, for no record of her death exists.

• **Caesar** was a black pirate. He was a member of Blackbeard's crew and became a favorite companion of the infamous pirate captain. He outlived his notorious leader, but only for a short time. In 1718 he was caught and hanged in Williamsburg, Virginia.

• Capt. **Richard Worley** may have been the most ambitious Carolina pirate. He began his pirate career by leaving New York Harbor in a small open boat, with eight crewmen and a stack of stolen muskets. He and his companions managed to capture a small ship, used it to overtake a larger vessel, and eventually worked themselves up to possession of a six-gun warship that required a crew of twenty-five. Despite his career advancement, Worley was captured off South Carolina and was hanged in Charleston.

• **Samuel Odell** may have suffered the oddest fate. He was captured by Blackbeard and forced to join the pirate's crew. The next day, on his first full day of piracy, Odell's ship was attacked by the South Carolina colonial navy, and Odell was wounded more than seven times in the battle. Somehow he survived to stand trial and was declared innocent. When released, he quietly disappeared.

• Pirate **Charles Vane** had a peculiar career. He gained a reputation plundering Spanish galleons in the Caribbean, then moved to the Carolina coast.

After looting a succession of ships, he sailed to Central America, where he was challenged by a French warship. He refused to do battle and so shamed his crew that they mutinied and set him adrift in a small boat. Stranded on an island, Vane was rescued by an old friend, who declared him a coward and turned him over to authorities for hanging.

• Capt. **William Lewis** was also undone by his crew. After a remarkable ten-year career of piracy off the Carolina coast, he was feared by all men of the sea, including other pirates. His reputation for ruthlessness became so fearsome that his crew decided he was in league with the devil and murdered him in his sleep.

• Perhaps the oddest pirate to roam the Grand Strand waters was **Stede Bonnet,** who was known as the Gentleman Pirate. The son of respectable English parents, he was given a good education, became a British army officer, and rose to the rank of major before he retired to a sugar plantation in Barbados. Although he was a prominent member of the island's aristocratic planter society, he decided to become a pirate in 1717, according to legend, to escape a nagging wife.

Bonnet knew little about the sea and less about piracy. Instead of stealing a ship and kidnapping a crew in pirate fashion, he bought a ship and hired a crew. He gave his ship a fierce-sounding name, the *Revenge,* but despite his posturing no one took him very seriously, including his crew. At one time during Bonnet's brief career, Blackbeard commandeered the *Revenge,* much to the relief of the ship's

Stede Bonnet, the Gentleman Pirate, was finally captured at Bonnet's Creek, just north of the Grand Strand.

crew. When Blackbeard returned Bonnet's ship to him, the Gentleman Pirate set about to make a name for himself. He developed a cruel streak and may have been the only pirate who really made his victims walk a plank. (Most pirates simply tossed unwanted victims over the side.)

After a bizarre battle off what is now Bonnet's Creek in the mouth of the Cape Fear River north of the Grand Strand, Bonnet was captured and put on trial in Charleston. He was convicted and sentenced to hang. He escaped but was recaptured, and after repeated pleas for clemency, Stede Bonnet was publicly hanged in Charleston in 1718 and was buried in the marsh below the low water mark.

• Of all the pirates who patrolled the Atlantic off today's Grand Strand, the most notorious was the bloodthirsty **Blackbeard.** His real name was Edward Teach or Edward Drummond. He was an Englishman from Bristol who served aboard a privateer in the Caribbean as a young man. He changed from privateer to pirate when he and a crew seized a well-built French merchant ship. They fitted it with no less than forty cannons, renamed it *Queen Anne's Revenge,* and began raiding the sea-lanes between the North American colonies and the Caribbean.

Blackbeard was a huge figure who wore a long, bushy black beard and was usually equipped with a brace of six pistols across his chest. Before battle he would plait his beard into pigtails onto which he would tie slow-burning artillery fuses. Just before facing the enemy he would light the fuses, which would send smoke curling around his beard, creating a dramatic and eerie appearance.

He earned a reputation for ferocity and daring when he fought and won a naval battle with a thirty-gun British man-of-war, becoming perhaps the only pirate in the Western Hemisphere to defeat the British Royal Navy. Commanding one pirate ship was not enough for Blackbeard; he assembled a squadron of pirate vessels in the early 1700s and turned them loose on merchant ships off the Carolina coast, terrorizing colonial shipping. He would strike a vessel or direct a series of captures, then retreat to his favorite hideaway: Ocracoke Island on North Carolina's Outer Banks.

His main target was the rich traffic from the flourishing young port of Charleston. In one raid on the port's shipping he captured a succession of nine ships and held hostage a group of passengers, including a prominent member of the colony's legislature. In a message to South Carolina Governor Robert Johnson, Blackbeard offered to spare the legislator and the other passengers in exchange for a large supply of medicine. If the governor failed to comply, Blackbeard warned, he would execute his hostages, then raid and sack Charleston. The governor called an emergency session of the legislature, which noted the absence of British warships in the port and voted to meet Blackbeard's demands. When the medicines were taken aboard his ship, Blackbeard freed his hostages and retreated to North Carolina.

In North Carolina Blackbeard reportedly enjoyed the protection of Gov. Charles Eden, who was rumored to be taking lucrative bribes. After his extortion of Charleston, Blackbeard received an official pardon from Eden, bought a luxurious house in Bath, and married a sixteen-year-old girlfriend. He entertained the governor and the leading citizens of the colony until his fortune dwindled and he returned to sea.

It was then Blackbeard ran afoul of Gov. Alexander Spotswood of Virginia, who believed

Blackbeard, the most notorious pirate of his day, wore smoking artillery fuses tied to his beard.

pirates should be hanged, not protected. Spotswood tired of hearing reports of plunderings by pirates off the coast of Virginia. He outfitted a force of warships manned by British sailors and sent them to Ocracoke Island with orders to destroy Blackbeard's headquarters.

Commanded by a brave and able officer, Lt. Robert Maynard, the squadron of ships from Virginia arrived off Ocracoke in November 1718 and immediately attacked Blackbeard and his pirates. It was a bloody boarding action that reached a climax when Blackbeard and Maynard faced each other in hand-to-hand combat. Every British seaman within range or reach of the infamous pirate took a shot at him or slashed at him with cutlasses, but Blackbeard seemed indestructible. Finally, after suffering twenty-five wounds, the giant pirate fell dead on the deck of his ship.

When Lieutenant Maynard returned to Virginia, Blackbeard's severed head dangled from the bowsprit of Maynard's warship. The most famous of all pirates was dead. Although others occasionally attacked shipping off the Grand Strand for several more decades, Blackbeard's death signaled an end to the pirate era. Eventually, the terror of the black flag became nothing more than a fearsome legend.

CHAPTER • FIVE

THE

EMPIRE BUILT

ON RICE

I STOPPED MY HORSE AND HELD MY breath," recalled a northern visitor to a South Carolina rice plantation. "I have hardly in all my life seen anything so impressively grand and beautiful."

In the eighteenth and nineteenth centuries such a reaction was typical of visitors to the heart of South Carolina's rice empire, the southern end of today's Grand Strand. From the marshlands near Garden City, down Waccamaw Neck, and around Winyah Bay, a dynasty of wealth and power flourished for more than a century and a half.

It was a kingdom built on rice, an empire that sprawled over thousands and thousands of acres. Each plantation was a principality of woodlands, waterways, rice fields, slave villages, gardens, and roads. Each was peopled by a monarch, the planter, and his subjects: slaves and overseers, field hands and artisans, children and parents, the young and the old.

Like palaces in a fairyland, shrouded in Spanish moss and surrounded by camellias and magnolias, giant houses loomed over the plantations. In front of each home flowed the river, slow-moving, silent, and somber. Spread out at the river's edge were the rice fields, cut by canals and worked by men on flatboats. Away from the big house was the slave village, with its rows of frame shacks, where smoke drifted from dozens of chimneys and children played in sandy streets. Behind the big house were the outbuildings: kitchens, tool sheds, barns, and threshing towers.

The front door faced the river, where transportation was easier and quicker. Old King's Highway was in the rear, with its sandy bogs and wagon ruts. From the highway visitors approached the big house on a carriage lane flanked by moss-draped live oaks. Surrounding the big house in princely splendor were cultivated English gardens highlighted by well-trimmed hedges, aromatic rose beds, and brilliant oleander. It was a realm of beauty, riches, and culture utilizing the institution of slavery, yet leaving behind an enduring legend of almost mystical majesty.

It all began with Henry Woodward, the man who brought rice to South Carolina.

In 1666, in a gleeful adventure of youth, Woodward booked passage on an English ship sent to explore the coast of South Carolina in preparation for the establishment of an English colony. After months on the Atlantic, the ship made landfall somewhere near modern Beaufort. The Englishmen explored the region and established friendly relations with the local Indians. When the explorers were ready to return home, the ship's captain called for a volunteer to remain behind with the tribe as a goodwill ambassador until the English colonists arrived. Woodward accepted the job, staying with the Indians in the South Carolina wilderness while his companions sailed away to England.

His career as a diplomat was brief. Soon after his ship left, he was captured by a Spanish expedition raiding the coast for Indian slaves. Englishmen were despised by the Spaniards, who imprisoned Woodward at Saint Augustine. Somehow he escaped and joined the crew of an English privateer, serving as the ship's surgeon as the vessel plundered Spanish merchant ships in the Caribbean.

Life aboard a privateer was perilous, but Woodward survived the raids and the sea battles, only to be shipwrecked on a Caribbean island during a hurricane. His exile was mercifully brief. Soon after he washed ashore, he was rescued by a passing English ship. In one of history's oddities, the ship that plucked him from the island was carrying the colonists who were to establish the English colony in South Carolina. Four years after being kidnapped by the Spaniards, Woodward was rescued by the very group he was supposed to have been waiting for.

They established their colony near modern Charleston in 1670, and it was there some fifteen years later that colonist Henry Woodward made the discovery that launched an empire. Sometime in the 1680s a sea captain, docked in Charleston, gave Woodward a bag of seed rice from Madagascar. Woodward experimented with the rice and found it would grow abundantly in the Carolina marshlands. Knowing the huge profits rice produced as an export to England, he shared the discovery with his fellow colonists.

His timing was perfect. At another time and in another place, the introduction of rice might have meant nothing. In seventeenth-century South Carolina, however, all the ingredients necessary for a rice empire were present: demand for the product, adequate labor, and proper natural resources. The British population demanded a large and steady diet of grain, the system of slavery prevalent in the colony provided the extensive labor necessary for rice production, and the water level on the South Carolina coast was ideal for rice cultivation.

Barely twenty years after Woodward planted his experimental bag of seed rice, South Carolina rice planters were complaining there were not enough ships in the colony to export the crop. Rice quickly became the colony's main product, replacing deerskins, Indian slaves, and lumber. By the American Revolution, South Carolina was one of the largest producers of rice in the world, and by 1850 the rice empire had made the South Carolina coast into one of the wealthiest and most influential regions in the nation.

Waccamaw Neck rice planters enjoyed an affluence matched
by few landowners in America.

The heart of the South Carolina rice empire was
Waccamaw Neck, the narrow, tapering peninsula
created by the Atlantic Ocean on the east and the
Waccamaw River on the west. In 1850 almost forty-
seven million pounds of rice were produced on

Waccamaw Neck and the other rice fields of George-town County, making the region the largest rice pro-ducer in the United States. The grain produced in the Georgetown region was also considered by many planters to be the best rice in the world. In Tidewater Virginia, tobacco plantations produced millionaires; on the Gulf Coast, sugar plantations created fortunes; throughout the southern sandhills and Piedmont, cotton was king; but no southern planter aristocracy surpassed the riches and power of the Waccamaw Neck rice planters.

The rice empire produced a lifestyle for a privi-leged few possibly unmatched in the nation. Rice planters traveled extensively, entertained lavishly, stocked their pantries with the finest wines, and hired English or northern tutors for their children. Their daughters were expected to continue their education at Charleston and Savannah finishing schools. Sons were sent to military academies, pres-tigious northern colleges, or revered institutions in England and Europe.

Planters and their families usually vacationed in cooler climates during the Carolina summer, when so many Low Country residents sickened and died from the mysterious fever that haunted the Deep South. Bad air and "swamp gases" were blamed for the illness, which eventually was found to originate with the malaria-carrying mosquitoes breeding in the swamps and marshes.

During the fever season planters and their fami-lies retired to summer homes in the South Carolina Piedmont or to the North Carolina mountains. Some took leisurely trips to the north, toured

Europe, or moved to their summer homes on the beach to seek the protection of the healthy ocean breeze. Overseers and the plantation's slave community were left to brave the fever and operate the plantation. The planters lived on their plantations during spring and early fall, when rice was planted and harvested. During the winter they often moved to Charleston, where many owned homes—the graceful expensive mansions on Tradd and Meeting streets and along the Battery. Rice profits from Waccamaw Neck were greatly responsible for making Charleston into what was often called "the richest, proudest city in the South."

Over generations, the rice planters intermarried and formed dynasties. The Georgetown County rice empire produced one signer of the Declaration of Independence, a succession of state leaders, several cabinet members and ambassadors, and some of the most powerful political brokers in the nation.

One of the wealthiest members of the rice empire was Plowden C. J. Weston, a Waccamaw Neck planter who presided over Hagley Plantation, a rich, sprawling estate on the Waccamaw River. Weston inherited a huge fortune from his father, who was descended from a line of rice planters. Educated at Harrow and Cambridge in England, Weston married into English aristocracy in 1847. The marriage infuriated his father, whose allegiance to the American Revolution had created a genuine dislike for Britons. The father consented to the match, however, and even made the trip to England to meet his son's in-laws and attend the wedding. But when the bride's father boasted of giving his

The Waccamaw Neck became the nation's center of rice production. *(Fields Prepared for Planting, by Alice Ravenel Huger Smith, Gibbes Museum of Art/Carolina Art Association)*

daughter seven thousand pounds as a wedding present, it was too much for the senior Weston.

"I'll give her seventy thousand pounds," he calmly remarked, "and a house in London and one in Geneva." Intimidated by such a display of wealth, the pompous Englishman ceased boasting. "I was going to do him ten better," Weston's father later disclosed, "no matter what he said."

Plowden C. J. Weston and his bride returned to the rice empire on the Waccamaw. There Weston became a memorable figure. His plantation produced immense wealth, enabling him to spend much time studying South Carolina history and to assemble a library valued at fifteen thousand dollars, a remarkable sum for the nineteenth century.

He spent another fortune to stock a cellar of the finest wines of Europe. He devoted much time to reading and study, becoming somewhat eccentric over the years. One of his favorite pastimes was jumping fully clothed into the Waccamaw.

When the War Between the States erupted, Weston joined the Georgetown Rifle Guards, a local militia unit, enlisting as a private despite his great wealth. While stationed on South Island near Georgetown during the war's early days, he bought weapons, uniforms, and equipment for all the soldiers of his company. He provided musicians for company parades and even supplied feasts of roast turkey for Sunday dinner in camp. Predictably, he was soon elected captain. One day in 1861 when two companies and an artillery unit were on a march near Hagley Plantation, Weston invited the entire force to his home for dinner. When the troops marched in, he gave a few orders, and soon all 163 soldiers were seated and served an elaborate multi-course meal, with fine china and silverware, and a succession of wines of the rarest vintage.

Another affluent rice planter was John Hyrne Tucker, who owned Willbrook and Litchfield plantations. Born into the rice culture in 1780, Tucker acquired thorough knowledge of rice cultivation from childhood. By the time he was an adult with plantations of his own, rice planting had become an obsession with him. He freely admitted that little else in life mattered to him beyond rice planting. Such single-minded devotion made him an expert at his profession, and in 1850 his property produced a remarkable one million pounds of rice.

Tragically scarred by smallpox as a child, Tucker was anything but a dashing figure. Yet he was noted for his ability to attract women, aided perhaps by his extensive fortune. He survived three wives and had no trouble acquiring a fourth.

The richest Waccamaw rice planter was Joshua John Ward, who owned six plantations totaling more than ten thousand acres. The largest slaveholder in the United States, he possessed more than eleven hundred slaves. Among his plantations were Brookgreen, Longwood, Springfield, Alderly, Prospect Hill, and Oryzantia. He also owned several summer homes and extensive property in Charleston. In 1850 he perfected a strain of rice called Carolina Golden Grain and was awarded a grand prize at the Paris Exposition. When he died in 1853, Ward was known as "the king of the rice planters."

It was by slavery that the rice empire flourished, and when slavery died, the empire died with it. As the seat of the southern rice empire, Waccamaw Neck and the rest of the Low Country formed the center of slavery in South Carolina. In the years before the Civil War, Georgetown County recorded the largest slave population in the United States. Of the 21,305 residents of Georgetown County in 1860, more than 18,000—approximately 85 percent—were slaves.

Although slavery would continue to exist in Africa and South America for decades to come, by 1850 the most perceptive planters could see that slavery was a vanishing institution in the Western world. Country by country, slavery was being abolished. By 1850 slavery was illegal in Great Britain and most of western Europe, the British West Indies, and many American states. The rice planters argued that their slaves fared better than they would have if they had lived in wild and pagan Africa and that slavery on southern plantations was a better life than what existed in the sweatshops and factories of the North and in England. Seeing the growing international trend toward the abolition of slavery, the rice planters tried to make the institution more humane, but their arguments and efforts were overtaken by the War Between the States.

A few small rice crops were still produced during the early twentieth century, but they were a vanishing reminder of the lost empire. *(Courtesy of Brookgreen Gardens)*

When the war ended and emancipation was enforced, the rice empire lost its labor force. After more than a century and a half of wealth and influence, the empire ceased to exist. For years to come, as late as the early twentieth century, some landowners tried to produce rice, but the rice empire was no more. Unable to maintain their property without huge profits, the surviving rice planters moved to their Charleston homes or entered other professions. Gradually the rice plantations fell into decay. The cultivated English gardens were reclaimed by Carolina forest. Most of the big houses on the river fell into disrepair and collapsed. The once bustling plantation wharves rotted and disappeared into the river, and the once busy rice fields were silent and abandoned.

Today visitors to the Grand Strand speed along Highway 17 through Waccamaw Neck, looking toward the beaches—unaware of the lost empire now swallowed by time and nature.

CHAPTER • SIX

THE

FOUNDING FATHER

WHO DISAPPEARED

FROM THE STONE STEPS IN FRONT OF HIS house at Peachtree Plantation, thirty-year-old Thomas Lynch, Jr., could see the muddy South Santee River flowing sluggishly through the rice fields toward the Atlantic. As he watched the lazy river, perhaps he thought about his health and the war he had helped create. He was a sick man this day in 1779, and the War of Independence was not going well for the Americans. Four years earlier, shortly after the fighting began, young Lynch had left the Georgetown region to help recruit troops for the American cause in North Carolina. There he caught the dreaded fever. Unlike many victims, he survived, but the fever left him weak and unhealthy, and the years of revolution had been hard and demanding in many ways.

Now, at his doctor's suggestion he and his wife, Elizabeth, were packing for a restful voyage to the south of France, where he hoped to relax and regain his good health. He knew the trip involved some danger. His ship would have to slip past the British coastal blockade. Then, after a brief stop in the West Indies, he would have to endure the long voyage across the Atlantic. Even so, he had decided to take the trip. Nothing had restored his health so far, and he hoped the mild climate, rest, and distance from the stress of war would restore his strength.

The Revolution was crucially important to him. It had begun in a swirl of excitement following the outbreak of hostilities near Boston. Everyone thought it would be a quick little war, that the British government would relent when the Americans demonstrated their willingness to fight. Instead, it had become a long and bloody conflict.

So much had happened since those early exciting days of drafting declarations and raising armies. They had declared their independence, but the boast was still only a defiant shout, a hope still to be realized on the field of war. For more than three years they had been fighting. Their strength and their tenacity had surprised the British commanders, who had predicted a quick end to the rebellion. Yet victory remained elusive. As always the American forces were outnumbered and on the defensive. Still, Lynch believed, if they could hold

Educated in Great Britain, Thomas Lynch, Jr., had the mind of an English barrister and the heart of a Carolina rice planter.

on, they could perhaps win and make American independence a reality.

The Lynch family had not been eager to break with the mother country. Looking at the murky South Santee, with its marshlands and live oaks, Lynch understood just how different America was from England. The colonists had conquered a hostile land far different from the country Englishmen knew. Americans were independent-minded. They wanted to press westward, to build a new land, and they did not want to be cramped and exploited by the politicians back in London who had no understanding of America. Even so, the Lynches chose independence reluctantly.

Lynch crossed the Atlantic and entered Eton when he was a boy of fifteen. After Eton came Cambridge University and the study of law at Middle Temple in London. He finished his education with the mind of an English lawyer but the heart of a South Carolina rice planter. Like the four generations before him, he would live the planter's life. His great-grandfather Jonack Lynch was the first. An Irish Catholic with roots in French aristocracy, Jonack immigrated to South Carolina in 1677, shortly after the colony was founded. He received property near Charleston and became a prosperous planter and a member of the colony's legislature.

Jonack's son, Thomas I, was also a planter and a legislator. He expanded the family lands to Georgetown. Thomas II, Lynch's father, inherited the family fortune, became a planter and legislator, and moved the family to the Santee River below Georgetown. Lynch's father built Hopsewee

Plantation on the north bank of the Santee. Lynch was born there in 1749, and he grew to adulthood knowing he would be heir to a rice plantation.

For the first thirteen years of his life, Lynch had gone to sleep at night in the big two-story house at Hopsewee. In the daytime he played along the banks of the North Santee, wandered into the kitchens out back, ran and jumped along the carriage lane behind the house, and accompanied his father to the slave village and the fields. In 1762 the family moved across the Santee delta to Peachtree Plantation, which overlooked the river opposite Hopsewee. Two years later Lynch left for England to receive the education proper for a rice planter.

In 1772, after almost a decade in England, he returned to Peachtree. That same year he married Elizabeth Shubrick, a planter's daughter, and became master of Peachtree. Two years later, like his ancestors, he sought a seat in South Carolina's colonial legislature. He was unsuccessful, but his political career was nurtured by the Revolution.

In 1774, during the political tensions that preceded the war, he was elected parish representative to the Provincial Congress of South Carolina, which was charged with sending delegates to the new Continental Congress in Philadelphia. The thirteen colonies were finally taking some unified action, sending delegates to organize a formal, continental protest against British oppression. Five South Carolinians had served in the first Continental Congress the previous fall, and one of them was Lynch's father. The senior Lynch was a veteran lawmaker who had served in the colony's legislature more than twenty years. He was the most influential political figure in the Georgetown region and was one of South Carolina's prominent leaders.

Although he initially opposed independence from Great Britain, Lynch's father was a vigorous supporter of colonial rights. He and the other delegates to the first Continental Congress had adopted a ringing declaration of rights calling for more autonomy from the government in London. The British leaders officially ignored the protest, garrisoned British troops in Boston to handle the hotheaded New Englanders, and waited for the colonists to make the next move.

A second Continental Congress was called in Philadelphia in 1775. The elder Thomas Lynch was again elected a delegate, and while he faced the crisis in Philadelphia, his son served in the provincial congress meeting in Charleston. In March of 1776 young Lynch received a message bearing tragic news: His father had suffered a cerebral hemorrhage in Philadelphia and was in grave condition.

In reaction to the news, the South Carolina Provincial Congress voted to increase the size of the colony's delegation to the Continental Congress and to send Lynch to Philadelphia as a sixth delegate. There he could assist his father and represent South Carolina. By the time Lynch reached Philadelphia, his father was better but was still unable to attend the congress. Lynch joined the South Carolina delegation meeting at Independence Hall and entered into the debate. Like his father and some of the other members of the delegation, Lynch was reluctant to establish an independent government. The concept

At the age of twenty-six, Thomas Lynch, Jr., joined John Hancock, Benjamin Franklin, and other Continental leaders in signing the Declaration of Independence. *(From the original painting, "Signing the Declaration of Independence," by Mort Künstler. Copyright 1986 Mort Künstler, Inc.)*

of a democratic republic troubled some of the aristocratic planters, who feared too much power in the hands of the people might lead to anarchy.

The Lynches and the rest of the delegation finally decided that independence was inevitable and voted for the adoption of the Declaration of Independence. The document was publicly released on 4 July 1776. When the delegates signed the declaration, Thomas Lynch, Sr., was too ill to sign, so a space was left for his signature to be added. Lynch signed with the rest of the South Carolina delegation and, at the age of twenty-six, became the fifty-second signer of the Declaration of Independence.

The Declaration was read to Washington's army. *(From the original painting, "Reading the Declaration of Independence to the Troops," by Mort Künstler. Copyright 1979 Mort Künstler, Inc.)*

Five months later, in December 1776, Lynch left Philadelphia with his ailing father, planning to take the elder Lynch to his home to rest and recover. Father and son got only as far as Annapolis, Maryland, where the elder Lynch suffered another cerebral hemorrhage and died. Lynch buried his father in Annapolis, and the space on the Declaration of Independence remained blank.

Back home at Peachtree, Lynch had no way of knowing whether his signature on the historic document would mark him as a patriot or brand him forever as a traitor. If he felt any elation over his participation in the famous declaration, it was overshadowed by heartache. His father was dead, and his own health had worsened. He decided to retire from active public life, and his return from Philadelphia marked the end of his brief political career. But as a signer of the Declaration of Independence he would acquire status in history far surpassing his prominent father.

As he prepared for his voyage to France, Lynch did not know how the great political drama he had helped create would end. He could not know that the British would soon invade South Carolina, capture Charleston, and occupy Georgetown. Nor could he foresee the victorious end of the Revolution and the establishment of a new nation, the United States of America. He probably never dreamed that generations of Americans would revere the Declaration of Independence that bore his signature.

Victory and fame as a founding father lay only two years ahead, but he would not see it. In

December of 1779 he and his wife left South Carolina for France and were lost at sea. Thomas Lynch, Jr., the fifty-second signer of the Declaration of Independence, disappeared forever at the age of thirty.

The young founding father from Georgetown vanished forever three years after signing the Declaration of Independence.

CHAPTER • SEVEN

THE

SWAMP FOX

OF THE REVOLUTION

THEY HURRIED THROUGH THE SWAMPS, guiding their horses around the thickets and looking over their shoulders for the enemy. A few of them wore uniforms, but most wore farmers' homespun. Some carried muskets. The rest were armed with shotguns. They were Marion's men, led by Francis Marion, a hard, elusive guerrilla leader of the American Revolution. This November day in 1780 they pounded across fields and splashed through swamps, pursued by a troop of seasoned British cavalry, the fearsome Green Dragoons. Known by the color of their distinctive tunics, the dragoons were commanded by Lt. Col. Banastre Tarleton and were under orders to hunt down and destroy Marion and his band of guerrillas.

The American Revolution was in its sixth year. The British had taken the war from the North to the Middle Atlantic states and, finally, to the South. They had defeated the Continental troops in Georgia and South Carolina and were moving to attack North Carolina. Marion, a lieutenant colonel in the Continental army, undermined the British plan. His troops, the only Continental force not killed, captured, or driven out of the South Carolina Low Country, intimidated the British loyalists and threatened British traffic on the road between Charleston and Camden. With ambushes and surprise attacks they had defeated Tories near the Little Pee Dee, at Blue Savannah, at Black Mingo Swamp, and at Tearcoat Swamp. Stealing out of the forest one night, Marion's fighters also captured a British escort and freed a large group of Continental prisoners of war.

Lord Charles Cornwallis's southern campaign, Britain's final effort to keep its grip on the colonies, was held back because of Marion, and Cornwallis issued orders for the destruction of the guerrilla leader and his men. Tarleton, a moody, bad-tempered officer whose brutality had earned him the name "Bloody Ban," took the assignment. Tarleton knew if Marion's scantily equipped soldiers could be trapped, or lured into making a stand, they would be no match for the Green Dragoons.

Tarleton planned an ambush at a farmhouse Marion and his troops frequently visited, but

Bold exploits in guerrilla war against the British made Francis Marion an American hero.

Marion detected the trap and retreated into the swamps before Tarleton could attack. The Green Dragoons gave chase but they could not keep up with Marion and his horsemen, who knew every trail and turn of their swampy homeland. Seven hours later and miles away in the swamp, an exhausted, frustrated Tarleton finally called a halt. He looked at his winded horsemen. They had not even caught sight of Marion, and Tarleton knew they never would. "Come on, my boys," he shouted, "let us go back. As for this damned old fox, the devil himself could not catch him."

Still deeper in the darkening forest, out of sight and hearing, Francis Marion led his men through the maze of swampland, unaware that his enemy had given him a historic nickname: the Swamp Fox of the Revolution.

Marion was an unlikely looking figure to become one of history's heroes. At the time of the American Revolution he was short, lean, and middle-aged, known for his remarkably dark eyes and hawklike nose. His uninspiring appearance was deceiving, however, for Marion possessed abilities that enabled him to mold undisciplined South Carolina farmers into a fearsome guerrilla force that kept the British army and the loyalist militia under almost constant attack. A superb horseman, Marion led his men out of the dense swampland, slashing at the enemy with surprise raids and disappearing like a shadow when pursued.

In battle he calmly directed the action, pointing his troops toward an enemy weakness or calling them back when they were overly threatened. Despite his

Lt. Col. Banastre Tarleton (*left*), commander of Britain's notorious Green Dragoons, gave Marion the epithet "Swamp Fox." Lord Cornwallis (*right*), commander of British forces in the South, saw his plans to subdue South Carolina frustrated by Marion and his men.

participation in battle, he so seldom drew his saber that it was said to have rusted in its scabbard.

Marion earned his fame as a soldier, but his childhood desire was to be a sailor. Born in the winter of 1732, a tiny, puny baby with deformed ankles and knees, he was the youngest of Gabriel and Ester Marion's six children. When Marion was six, the family moved from Marion's birthplace in Saint John's Parish to a modest plantation at Belle Isle, on the banks of Winyah Bay near Georgetown. As a child watching merchant ships sail into the bay from the Atlantic, bound for the docks of Georgetown, Marion dreamed of a life at sea.

When he was fifteen, he persuaded his parents to let him join the crew of a schooner sailing for the West Indies. His career as a seaman was brief. On the return voyage to Georgetown the schooner was rammed and sunk by a whale, leaving young Marion in a lifeboat with six men and a dog. Before the drifting seamen were rescued, two men had died and the survivors had made a meal of the dog. By the time his ordeal was ended and he was safely home, Marion had lost all desire to be a sailor.

His father died when Marion was about eighteen. As the only unmarried son, he remained at home with his widowed mother and assumed charge of the little family plantation. He stayed in the rice country of Georgetown for the next five years, then moved with two of his brothers back to Saint John's Parish. There he began his career as a soldier in 1756, when he joined the South Carolina militia during the French and Indian War.

He first saw the smoke of battle at age twenty-nine, when he served in the 1761 campaign against the Cherokees. The expedition destroyed fifteen Indian villages and left Marion with mixed emotions. Years later he recalled the concern he felt upon seeing fresh footprints of playful Indian children in a cornfield he and other soldiers were setting afire. Yet despite his misgivings, Marion, a militia lieutenant, earned a reputation for coolness and courage under fire.

After the French and Indian War ended in 1763, he resumed the planter's life and ten years later bought Pond Bluff Plantation on the Santee River near Eutaw Springs. There he prospered and in

1775 was elected to the South Carolina Provincial Congress, which sent delegates to the Continental Congress meeting in Philadelphia.

A few months later, when the dispute between the colonies and Britain turned into war, the Continental Congress called on South Carolina and the other newly formed states to provide troops for a national army. Marion was elected captain in one of the new regiments, the Second South Carolina Line. After the battle of Sullivan's Island in 1776, which drove the British out of Charleston Harbor, he was promoted to lieutenant colonel. He spent the next three years on duty around Charleston; then in 1779 he commanded his regiment in an unsuccessful assault on Savannah, where his troops suffered high casualties.

Fortunately for the Continental cause, Marion was not in Charleston in May 1780 when the British returned in force and captured the city. He had left Charleston two months earlier after being injured at a regimental party at the home of an army officer. The party became a drinking bout, and Marion, who was a teetotaler, decided to leave. His host protested, however, and locked all the doors. Undeterred, Marion marched upstairs, raised a window, and jumped from the second floor. He landed badly, severely sprained an ankle, and went home to his plantation to recuperate. When Charleston's Continental garrison surrendered to the British, Marion was home mending his ankle. He remained free to continue the war—thanks to an aversion to alcohol.

After seizing Charleston the British moved inland and shattered the Continental forces at the battle of Camden. The day before the action Marion had been sent east to command the patriot militia between the Santee and the Pee Dee rivers, so he again escaped defeat and capture.

For months after the battle of Camden, Marion and his militiamen were the only opposition to the British army in South Carolina. From the fields, forests, and swampland of South Carolina's Low Country, Marion mustered the sons and grandsons of Huguenot, Scotch-Irish, and English immigrants. They were rugged, self-reliant men who had wrested small farms from the wilderness. They were comfortable on horseback, and they knew the bogs and trails of the dense swampland. They had learned how to endure hardship, and they handled a musket with casual skill.

Unlike their British opponents, Marion's guerrillas had no quartermaster corps or supply lines, so they improvised. Each man was responsible for supplying his rations and his horse. They fashioned saw blades into swords and molded their musket balls from pewter plates. Their numbers ranged from forty to four hundred, and they seldom had enough men to fight a conventional battle. Instead, they struck with stealth, often attacking at night. When pursued, they would outdistance the enemy in the gloomy swamps, then stage an ambush, cutting up their pursuers in a crossfire and sending the survivors fleeing.

The backwoods fighting was savage, yet Marion somehow maintained surprising discipline among his troops. As an officer of regulars in Charleston, he had marched his men to weekly church services

The Revolution in South Carolina became a bitter civil war that pitted neighbor against neighbor.

and had punished soldiers who appeared on parade with unkempt beards and uncombed hair. Living in the swamps, Marion's men were not expected to attend church services or get regular haircuts, but Marion kept them from committing brutalities common to guerrilla warfare. Although quiet, moody, and reflective, Marion inspired loyalty and obedience.

Between raids Marion and his men retreated to swampland hideaways like Snow's Island, which lies in the Pee Dee River a few miles west of today's Grand Strand. Hidden there among the cypress and thickets, living off wild game and sweet potatoes, Marion planned his raids.

The British hoped to subdue South Carolina and conquer the new American states one by one until the rebellion was suppressed. But Marion's bold fighters were so successful—striking British outposts, disrupting supply lines, and cutting communications—that the British strategy was stalled in South Carolina. It was this success that drove the British high command to dispatch Tarleton and his ruthless Green Dragoons in pursuit of Marion.

Tarleton was a likely choice to go after the Swamp Fox. At the Waxhaw massacre near Camden, he and his British cavalry had earned the hatred of South Carolinians by butchering disarmed Continental troops after they had surrendered. In his campaign to catch Marion, Tarleton drove his men relentlessly, setting traps, dispatching patrols, and stumbling through mud, moss, and mosquitoes in futile pursuit. It was all for nothing. Marion always eluded him. In frustration Tarleton and his horsemen destroyed grain mills, burned homes, and killed livestock along the Black and Pee Dee rivers. Once Tarleton dined in the home of a prominent South Carolina widow, then burned her barn—after driving all the livestock into it. Adding to her humiliation, he had her husband's body pulled from its grave.

Despite Tarleton's ruthless warfare, Marion remained free and at war with the British. Finally,

British troops frequently questioned and harassed Low Country residents who were loyal to the Continental cause.

when Continental victories elsewhere enabled Washington to shift some of his forces, reinforcements were sent to South Carolina, and Marion's guerrillas no longer had to face the British alone.

Appointed brigadier general of militia in 1780, Marion caused the British even more grief. He took a force of militia and Continental regulars and captured two important British outposts, Fort Watson and Fort Motte. He raided Georgetown and captured the port's British commander in his bed one night. Later he occupied the town when the British evacuated it. In the important American victory at Eutaw Springs, Marion played a prominent role as commander of the militia force supporting the Continental army.

Finally, in 1782, the year after the British southern strategy and hopes for victory collapsed with Cornwallis's defeat at Yorktown, Marion was able to stand at the edge of Charleston Harbor and

Cornwallis's surrender to Washington's army at Yorktown in 1781 followed a frustrating campaign in the Carolinas, where his forces failed to capture the elusive Swamp Fox. *(From the original painting, "Surrender at Yorktown," by Mort Künstler. Copyright 1986 Mort Künstler, Inc.)*

watch the British sail away for England. The Revolution had ended in victory for the Americans, and Francis Marion's grueling war with the British became history.

After the war Marion finally married. He retained a command in the state militia and served in the state senate. His last years, however, were spent at his cherished plantation experimenting with methods of growing indigo. There in the heart of the South Carolina Low Country he had fought so hard to protect, the old soldier died quietly on 26 February 1795 at the age of sixty-three.

At his death Marion's contribution to the War of Independence was largely unrecognized outside of South Carolina. His dream was to be remembered for advances made in the cultivation of indigo. He never imagined becoming a national military hero. A decade after Marion's death, however, an itinerant biographer named Mason Weems somehow acquired the wartime memoirs of Marion's most trusted officer, Col. Peter Horry, and produced a book called *The Life of General Francis Marion.* An earlier biography of George Washington by Weems had become a national bestseller, and the author's romantic treatment of Horry's memoirs made Francis Marion into an American hero.

Hungry for a national identity and inspired by the details of Marion's remarkable campaign against the British, the American public responded to the story of the Swamp Fox with a national outpouring of appreciation. Throughout the young, expanding nation, Francis Marion was honored by its citizens. From South Carolina to Kansas, from

Alabama to Iowa, Marion's name was given in honor to an amazing variety of items—towns, counties, lakes, colleges, forests, and countless babies—all christened Marion in tribute to the famous soldier who had dreamed of becoming a sailor.

CHAPTER • EIGHT

WASHINGTON SLEPT HERE —REALLY!

PULLED BY FOUR HORSES, THE OFFICIAL carriage of the president of the United States rolled along the rutted road through the piney forest between Wilmington and the South Carolina line. King's Highway in 1791 was a lonely, sandy lane through woods and thickets along the Atlantic coast. The bumpy, desolate road had seldom been used by such an elegant procession.

Four uniformed soldiers led the parade, followed by the president's carriage and a baggage wagon. Pulling the carriage was a team of immaculately groomed and superbly trained horses. Riding atop the coach with the driver were two neatly dressed footmen. Two servants and a presidential assistant accompanied the procession. The gleaming white coach was equipped with the rare luxuries of glass windows and venetian blinds. Its doors were decorated with a colorful coat of arms that marked the carriage's occupant as the most famous American of the day: George Washington, the first president of the United States of America.

Washington entered South Carolina along the Grand Strand at 12:30 P.M., Wednesday, 27 April 1791. Only two years earlier, on the balcony of Federal Hall in New York City, he had taken the oath of office as president. Now he had come south to meet the citizens of the new nation that he, more than anyone else, had forged into being.

Born in 1732 as the eldest son of Virginia planter Augustine Washington, he spent his early childhood on a Virginia tobacco plantation. When he was eleven years old, his father died, leaving his widow with ten thousand acres of land, fifty slaves, and six children. Young Washington assumed a man's responsibilities and eventually he yearned for independence. As a teenager, he begged his mother to give him permission to join the British navy, but she refused. Instead, he became a land surveyor at age fifteen, trudging through the wilds of western Virginia with a surveying team. He became an accomplished surveyor and at age seventeen he was appointed surveyor for Culpepper County, Virginia. He bought his first property that year and acquired a love for the land that would eventually make him one of America's largest landowners.

As a young man he visited the Caribbean island of Barbados, where he contracted smallpox. He survived the disease, but he never again left his native land. At age twenty, he inherited from his half brother the Mount Vernon plantation on the wide Potomac River. At age twenty-one, he became a major in the Virginia militia. A year later, under orders from the governor of Virginia, he led a force of militia to the forks of the Ohio River near modern Pittsburgh in an attempt to defend Virginia's western border from the French. He won a skirmish with French troops but later had to surrender a crude fort he had hastily built nearby. Washington narrowly escaped death the next year when the British army tried to force the French from the same site. When Gen. Edward Braddock, the commander of the British forces in the thirteen colonies, led his red-clad troops into an ambush engineered by the French and their Indian allies, Braddock and almost one thousand of his troops were shot down in the thick woods. Washington brought the survivors to safety.

In the French and Indian War that followed, Washington rose to the rank of colonel in the militia and gained experience that would be valuable to him in the American Revolution. During the war, in 1759, he married the widow Martha Custis and acquired a dowry of wealth and property, along with two children from Martha's earlier marriage. He would have no children of his own. He was elected to the Virginia House of Burgesses where he learned about politics, but his greatest joy came from managing Mount Vernon. There he experimented with new

As a lieutenant colonel of colonial troops in the French and Indian War, Washington learned the realities of war.

crops and livestock breeding while enjoying the lifestyle of a southern planter.

Although reserved and dignified, he was not a solemn, colorless aristocrat. He loved horses and hunting, working in the soil of Mount Vernon, and reading books on farming and business, but he seldom read anything else. He enjoyed socializing, and at plantation parties he had been known to remain on the dance floor until the music ended or morning dawned.

On the eve of the American Revolution, Washington was elected as a Virginia delegate to the First Continental Congress in Philadelphia, where he urged the other delegates to prepare for war, which he believed was unavoidable. When the tensions in Boston exploded into warfare between the New England militia and the British army, the Continental Congress created a national army and Washington was unanimously chosen as general in chief.

Commanding what the British considered nothing but a rabble in arms, Washington caused the Redcoats to evacuate Boston in 1776, but he was forced into an awkward retreat when the British invaded New York City several months later. He took an inexperienced, poorly equipped army across the frozen Delaware River on Christmas night to launch a victorious surprise attack on enemy forces at Trenton, New Jersey, then scored another quick win at Princeton.

Outmaneuvered by a much larger British army, he was unable to keep the British from occupying Philadelphia in 1777. The Continental Congress evacuated to nearby York, while the British turned Independence Hall into a prison and hospital. A key victory in New York at the battle of Saratoga kept the American cause alive, as Washington took the main army into winter camp at Valley Forge

Washington led the Continental army to eventual victory over the British. When grateful countrymen wanted to make him king of the United States, he refused. *(From the original painting, "Washington at Carlisle," by Mort Künstler. Copyright 1989 Mort Künstler, Inc.)*

near Philadelphia. It was a crucial winter for Washington: His troops gained vital training from foreign advisers and marched out of Valley Forge as a disciplined army—to learn that the French were joining the war against the British.

The British withdrew from Philadelphia back to New York City where Washington spent the next three years of the war trying to contain them. At the same time he fended off invasions by secondary British forces in the South. Lord Charles Cornwallis invaded South Carolina but was unable to subdue the state. He eventually marched his army into North Carolina, then moved north into Virginia and established a base on the long, vulnerable peninsula below Williamsburg.

When Washington learned that Cornwallis had isolated his army at Yorktown, he secretly put his troops on a hard forced march from New York to Virginia, where he attacked Cornwallis with the aid of a large French army and support from French warships. On 19 October 1781, surrounded and unable to escape, Cornwallis surrendered his army of seven thousand men to Washington.

Although a peace treaty would not be signed for two more years, the war was over and Washington had won. Some Americans wanted to make him king of America, but he resisted the suggestion and exercised his influence to lead the states toward an orderly, democratic republic.

Washington resigned his commission at war's end and returned to Mount Vernon. His country-men refused to let him go. When the Articles of Confederation failed to properly govern the young nation, Washington agreed to preside over the Constitutional Convention that drafted the Constitution of the United States and created a strong national government. Two years later, in 1789, he was unanimously elected as the nation's first president.

He spent the first two years of his first administration organizing the new constitutional government, developing foreign relations, and trying to bring order to the new nation's chaotic finances. The country's first census in 1790 reported four million Americans spread from New England to Georgia. In 1791, Washington decided it was time for him to get out of the capital, meet his citizens, and see how the nation fared. He organized two tours, one of the North and one of the South, and he decided to go south first.

He arrived at South Carolina's Grand Strand a month after he left Philadelphia, which was then the nation's capital. His first impression of the Grand Strand was less than enthusiastic. "Sand and pine barrens—with very few inhabitants," he wrote in his diary. The president's first meal in South Carolina was taken in the home of James Cochran, a veteran of the Revolution who lived in a modest house near Little River. Washington spent his first night on the Grand Strand with another veteran, Jeremiah Vareen, who operated a rural inn on King's Highway near the state line. Washington tried to pay for his lodging, but Vareen was honored to have the president as his guest and refused payment.

The famous fifty-nine-year-old leader whom Vareen watched board the coach the next morning

Instead of fame and political office, Washington—a devout Christian—wanted most to be a planter at his beloved Mount Vernon.

As the nation's first president, Washington chose to
visit the states in person.

was an impressive figure, six feet, two inches tall
and powerfully built. He was described as noble-
looking, with a calm face and a measured, dignified
charm.

Vareen escorted the president's carriage to
Singleton Swash at the site of today's Dunes Golf
and Beach Club in northern Myrtle Beach.
Apparently on Vareen's advice, the president left
King's Highway, crossed Singleton Swash, and
traveled down the beach, which was a smoother
ride than the rutted, bumpy King's Highway.

Vareen timed the crossing of the swash with low tide, which merited a notation in Washington's diary. "Mr. Vareen piloted us across the Swash," the president wrote, "which at high water is impassable and at times is dangerous, onto the long beach of the ocean."

The "long beach" the president described would one day attract millions of sunbathers, but as his coach rolled along the edge of the surf, Washington found only a deserted, picturesque strip of sand dunes, sea oats, and seagulls. The presidential coach rolled along the beach for sixteen miles until an inlet required the driver to turn back onto King's Highway. After traveling five miles farther, the president's party stopped for dinner at the home of George Pawley, a veteran of the Revolution who lived at Pawley's Island. Back on the road in the afternoon, Washington had traveled only a few more miles down Waccamaw Neck when a man appeared and waved down the entourage.

He introduced himself as Dr. Henry Collins Flagg, a former surgeon in the Continental army and now the master of nearby Brookgreen Plantation. Flagg invited Washington to spend the evening at Brookgreen and the president accepted.

There, among the live oaks overlooking the Waccamaw, he sampled the hospitality of a stately Low Country rice plantation. He also met a namesake. Dr. Flagg had married Rachel Moore Allston, the widow of an army officer, and her son by her first marriage was named Washington Allston in honor of the president. The boy, who was then age eleven, lived with his mother and stepfather at

The president left Philadelphia in April 1791 for his southern tour, which brought him through the South Carolina Grand Strand.

Brookgreen. Years later he would become one of America's best-loved nineteenth-century artists.

On Friday, 29 April, after a night beside the Waccamaw, Washington said early good-byes to the Flaggs and was driven down the peninsula to have breakfast with the region's most prominent planter, William "King Billy" Alston. Known for his wealth and influence, Alston owned several plantations, and Clifton was his showplace. Even Washington, who was familiar with wealth and affluent homes, was impressed by the splendor of Clifton Plantation. In his diary, Washington described it: "His house is large, new and elegantly furnished. It stands on a sand hill, high for this country, with his rice fields below, the contrast of which with the lands back of it, and the sand and piney barrens through which we passed, is scarcely to be believed."

Waiting to meet Washington at Clifton were three prominent South Carolinians—Maj. Gen. William Moultrie, Brig. Gen. John Rutledge, and Col. William Washington. Moultrie had led the defense of Charleston against the British in 1776, driving away the British fleet from a fort made of palmetto logs, the fort that gave South Carolina its name as the Palmetto State. He had served a term as governor of the state after the war and now was preparing to seek the office again.

Meeting Washington was a great moment for young John Rutledge, a devoted admirer of the president. He was a brigadier general in the state militia and the son of a state supreme court justice. Only twenty-five years old, he was already making a name for himself in his state. Four years earlier at a dinner party in London, he had silenced conversation by rebuking a prominent English gentleman who made a comment critical of Washington.

William Washington received the most intimate greeting from the president. A native Virginian who resided in Charleston, he had come to South Carolina as a Continental officer during the war. After a distinguished military career, William had married a planter's daughter. He had a special reason for wanting to meet the president: his grandfather and Washington's grandfather were brothers.

After an entertaining visit with the three South Carolinians, the president was shown around Clifton Plantation by King Billy, who welcomed Washington in regal style. On Saturday morning

King Billy escorted Washington to a decorated barge that took the president down the Waccamaw River to Georgetown. Arriving at the port docks, Washington was escorted to the town market, where he was honored by an artillery salute. He then inspected the Georgetown Light Infantry, a militia unit, which stood at attention in freshly pressed uniforms.

At the Georgetown home of Benjamin Allston, Washington was welcomed by speeches from local citizens and a committee of Masons, then he dined as the guest of honor at a public dinner. He repeatedly raised his glass to toasts by local residents who saluted the nation, the government, France, Lafayette, and "Our Illustrious President." That afternoon Washington presided over a tea party hosted by fifty Georgetown women.

Finally, after four days on the South Carolina Grand Strand, Washington climbed aboard his handsome coach on Sunday morning, 1 May 1791, and rolled out of Georgetown, bound for Charleston and Savannah. Although unimpressed with the "pine barrens" along King's Highway, Washington was enchanted with the beauty and culture of the Waccamaw Neck rice empire. "It was a fairyland," he told a Charleston woman, recalling the scenery and splendor of Clifton Plantation.

One minor frustration marked the president's visit to the Grand Strand: He could not properly pronounce the name "Waccamaw." In the diary of his journey, Washington noted that he had crossed the "Waggamau River."

CHAPTER • NINE

THE

MISSING

BEAUTY

THE SOUTH CAROLINA GOVERNOR, JOSEPH Alston, sat in the shadows of his wife's bedroom and wept. These days he returned to The Oaks, his plantation on the Waccamaw River, only to grieve. It was the home of his dreams, the mansion he had built for his bride, filled with memories of the son they had adored. Now both wife and son were gone, and he was left alone.

Her bedchamber was just as she had left it two months earlier. Her clothes still hung in the wardrobe. Her favorite books remained where she had placed them. On the floor the toys their cherished son so enjoyed lay where he had left them.

Joseph Alston had met Theodosia Burr far away from the rice fields of the Waccamaw, while visiting New York City. She lived there with her father for part of each year. Alston was enchanted with New York, and the city in 1800 was even more dazzling when he was with Theodosia.

He had never known a woman like Theodosia. A striking beauty with dark hair and dark eyes, she shunned the frivolity fashionable among the young women of her day, and her grace, poise and intelligence made her seem much older than eighteen. She possessed a remarkable variety of talents. Fluent in French, Latin, and classical Greek, she was a skilled musician and a graceful dancer. Proficient in mathematics and English composition, she was also keenly informed on current events and the political issues of the day. Her social graces were flawless. At fourteen she had acted as hostess of a large dinner party in the absence of her father, entertaining an array of guests that included political figures, an Indian chief, and the Catholic bishop of New York.

Her remarkable education and social skills were the products of intense, devoted attention from her father, Aaron Burr. A leading figure in the American Revolution, Burr was a famous New York lawyer, U.S. senator, and a presidential candidate who would soon be elected vice president of the United States. His daughter was the most coveted belle of New York society and was eagerly sought by young men of wealth and influence.

New York and Albany society gossips were shocked when they learned that Theodosia Burr would marry Joseph Alston of South Carolina's Waccamaw region. The state's political power was respected in New York, and young Alston was heir to a rice planting fortune, but Theodosia's acquaintances were still stunned by her choice of an unknown young man from the faraway south over the many available bachelors of New York. Theodosia's father must have arranged the marriage to get money from the rice empire for some of his political schemes, they whispered. Even if Joseph Alston was rich, they chattered, he was also "vain and silly," and some thought him "ugly and ill-tempered."

Theodosia saw him differently. "God knows how delighted I shall be when in your arms," she once wrote him. Like Theodosia, he was a remarkable young person. His father was William "King Billy" Alston, the wealthiest rice planter of the Waccamaw empire. Joseph Alston had received an education similar to Theodosia's. As a child he had been instructed by private tutors, and at sixteen he entered Princeton University. Three years later, at nineteen, he was admitted to the South Carolina bar as a practicing attorney. He inherited The Oaks, one of the showplace plantations of Waccamaw. When he met Theodosia, he was preparing for a political career.

They were married in Albany on 2 February 1801. She was eighteen and he was twenty-two. She adored her new husband and happily sailed for the South, but she admitted fear of the mysterious killer fever that haunted the South Carolina coast. On their honeymoon they attended the inauguration of

Aaron Burr (*left*) was famous and controversial: the survivor of a duel with Alexander Hamilton and a vice president of the United States who was later tried for treason. Theodosia Burr Alston (*right*), Burr's daughter, was the belle of New York society when she married Joseph Alston, a wealthy Waccamaw Neck rice planter. (*Yale University Library*)

Thomas Jefferson as president and Theodosia's father as vice president. Under the electoral system of the day, Jefferson and Burr had tied in the election, and the House of Representatives was forced to pick a winner. After thirty-six ballots they chose Jefferson by one vote.

From Washington, the new capital on the Potomac, the newlyweds moved to the Waccamaw where Joseph built a mansion overlooking the river. A year later Joseph was elected to the South Carolina house of representatives, and for the next ten years he and Theodosia seemed to live an idyllic existence. He would travel to Columbia for the legislative sessions but would spend most of his time at The Oaks or nearby at the family house on the beach. They traveled frequently and enjoyed the grand style of the South Carolina rice empire.

A year after the wedding, Theodosia gave birth to a son whom the couple named Aaron Burr Alston, in honor of Theodosia's father. A lively and talented child, young Aaron made The Oaks his playground and became an object of adoration for his parents and grandfather.

Life for Theodosia and Joseph was marred, however, by Theodosia's poor health and her father's controversial reputation. As she had feared, Theodosia did not adapt well to the warm and humid climate. Her health worsened after the birth of their son, and nothing seemed to produce long-term improvement.

Although Theodosia came to South Carolina respected as the daughter of the vice president of the United States, the relationship became a liability as Burr came to be viewed as one of the great villains of the day by many Americans. Argumentative and caustic, he lost the support of his party and was replaced as the vice presidential nominee after one term in office. He went home to Albany and ran for governor of New York but lost.

The real controversy came when he challenged Alexander Hamilton, the former secretary of the treasury, to a duel. The two men were bitter political rivals, and Burr blamed his political defeats on Hamilton, a leader of the opposing Federalist party. The feud spilled onto the pages of the nation's newspapers, and Burr invited Hamilton to settle their differences at gunpoint. On 11 July 1804, in a

New Jersey field, Burr and Hamilton faced each other with loaded pistols. Hamilton fired and missed, then was shot dead by Burr. The death of Hamilton, one of the Founding Fathers, unleashed a storm of condemnation on Burr.

Three years later he was the center of an even greater national spectacle when he was placed on trial for treason. For reasons never fully revealed Burr allegedly tried to recruit an army to establish a monarchy in the southwest from American and Mexican territories. His bizarre plan collapsed when he was betrayed by key conspirators. He was tried in federal court in Richmond, Virginia. By his side at the trial was Theodosia, who became Burr's most devoted defender. Had his plans for empire worked, Burr reportedly would have made himself emperor with Theodosia as first lady, Joseph Alston as head of nobility, and grandson Aaron Burr Alston as heir to the throne. Burr was acquitted on a technicality and returned to New York, accompanied by Theodosia. Soon afterward she returned to South Carolina, and Burr went to Europe in self-imposed exile.

Back home at The Oaks, Theodosia spent much of her time raising money for her father, who was still trying to enlist support for his western empire. Some of Burr's accusers claimed Joseph Alston invested large sums in Burr's conspiracy, but Alston denied the charges. Despite Theodosia's efforts, Burr was unable to recruit enough support for his scheme and finally returned to New York City in 1812.

To his surprise Theodosia was not there to meet him. Instead, a letter from The Oaks awaited him.

In it he learned that tragedy had struck Joseph and Theodosia. Ten-year-old Aaron Burr Alston had died of the fever.

"That boy on whom all rested," Joseph wrote to Burr, "our companion, our friend—he who was to have transmitted down the mingled blood of Theodosia and myself—he who was to have redeemed all your glory and shed new luster on our families—that boy, at once our happiness and our pride, is taken from us—is dead."

Shortly before his son died, Joseph Alston had won a heated campaign for governor of South Carolina. Now the new thirty-three-year-old governor viewed his victory as meaningless. The child's death was even harder on Theodosia. Her fragile health worsened, and she suffered from severe depression. Joseph agreed that Theodosia should visit her father, hoping she would recover in a colder climate and different surroundings.

Burr sent a New York doctor named Timothy Green to escort Theodosia; Joseph could not leave South Carolina. He was organizing his new administration, and the newly erupted War of 1812 had produced a torrent of duties for the youthful governor. He consented for Theodosia to travel to New York with Dr. Green and promised to join her later.

The war had restricted sea traffic, so Dr. Green considered himself fortunate to book passage for himself and Theodosia on the *Patriot,* a former American warship sailing from Georgetown. The schooner's guns were stored under deck, and she was under the command of an old Yankee sailing master. Green thought the *Patriot's* accommodations

Theodosia was honored by a gala going-away party in this Georgetown house before she disappeared.

(Paige Sawyer Photography)

were undignified, but she was the only vessel going to New York, and Theodosia, deep in grief, was eager to leave.

It was a bright winter day when Theodosia left. Sunlight sparkled on the murky waters on Winyah Bay, and a light breeze whispered in from the ocean. The *Patriot* pulled away from the Georgetown dock just after noon on Thursday, 31 December 1812. Joseph Alston was on board with Dr. Green and Theodosia. He planned to sail with his wife as far as the entrance to the bay, where he would board the accompanying pilot boat and return to Georgetown. He could have said good-bye at the town dock, but he wanted to go as far as possible with Theodosia.

Opposite the new lighthouse on North Island, where Winyah Bay meets the Atlantic, the young governor embraced his wife and promised to join her in New York as soon as his duties would allow. Aboard the pilot boat returning to port, he watched the ship enter the whitecaps of the Atlantic, then disappear over the horizon. Joseph Alston would never see his cherished Theodosia again.

A voyage from Georgetown to New York normally took six days. After two weeks without a letter from Theodosia, Joseph began to worry. Perhaps the *Patriot* had been driven into port by bad weather, he told himself, or perhaps she had docked somewhere for repairs. As the days passed with no word from Theodosia, he became distraught. He wrote Burr in New York, who confirmed that the ship had not arrived as scheduled. Hoping fervently that Theodosia would arrive late, Joseph poured his fears into a letter to her that he mailed to Burr.

"Another mail and still no letter!" he wrote. "I hear, too, rumors of a gale off Cape Hatteras the beginning of the month! The state of my mind is dreadful. I shall count the hours til noon tomorrow. If I do not hear then, there will be no hope til Tuesday. To feelings like mine, what an interval! May God grant me one word from you tomorrow. All I have left of heart is yours."

Three weeks after the *Patriot's* departure, Joseph began to lose hope. "Forebodings!" he wrote Burr. "Wretched, heart-rendering forebodings distract my mind. I may no longer have a wife, and yet my impatient restlessness addresses her a letter. Tomorrow will be three weeks since our separation and not one line. Gracious God!"

Finally, one month after he said good-bye to Theodosia, Joseph gave up hope of ever seeing her again. "I have heard nothing from the schooner or my wife," he wrote Burr in desperation. "I have been prey of feelings which you only can imagine. When I turned from the grave of my boy I deemed myself no longer vulnerable. Misfortune could have no other blow for me. I was wrong."

Joseph Alston never recovered from the loss of Theodosia. For months after her disappearance he would leave the governor's office in Columbia, return to The Oaks, and sit silently in Theodosia's undisturbed bedroom. His deep grief led to poor health, and three years later, while traveling to Columbia, he was stricken by a seizure. He was taken to Charleston, where he died several months later. His final request to Aaron Burr was for a portrait of Theodosia.

Theodosia's fate remains a mystery. When the *Patriot* failed to arrive in New York, Burr engineered a search of ships and ports from New York to Nassau, but no trace of the *Patriot* was found. Investigators concluded that the *Patriot* had foundered in a storm off Cape Hatteras, "the Graveyard of the Atlantic," and had gone down when the old warship's heavy cannon shifted to one side.

Years later, however, a series of deathbed statements uttered by former pirates offered a different story of the *Patriot's* fate. Beginning in the 1830s and continuing sporadically for thirty more years, aging, dying seamen along the southern coast from North Carolina to Alabama confessed to a similar story: The *Patriot* had been captured by pirates. In 1848 one old man said on his deathbed that he had

Gov. Joseph Alston never recovered from his wife's disappearance. He died soon after and was buried in the family plantation cemetery. *(Paige Sawyer Photography)*

helped murder the passengers and crew of the *Patriot*. One of the victims, he recalled, was a strikingly beautiful woman who had been offered her life if she would be mistress to the pirate captain. Instead, the defiant beauty had chosen death. He could not remember her name, the dying pirate said, but it was something like "Odessa Burr Alston."

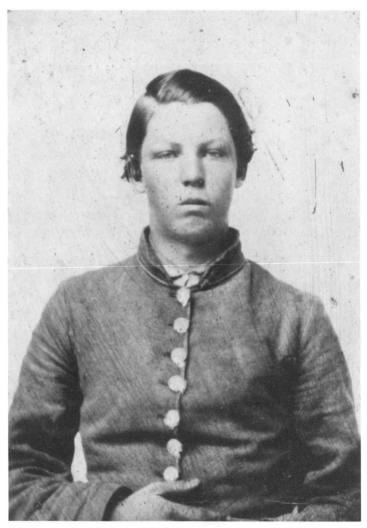

Like young Hilliard Todd of Conway, most men of fighting age from Horry County joined the Confederate army to fight for southern independence. One of five brothers to enlist, Hilliard alone survived the war. *(Courtesy of Dennis Todd)*

CHAPTER • TEN

"TAKING
UP THE
CAUSE"

YOUNG HILLIARD TODD DID NOT LOOK LIKE
a soldier. At age eighteen, he had the smooth-faced
look of a schoolboy. When the War Between the
States began to draw other young men away from
the farms and families around Conwayboro, young
Hilliard Todd decided to go to war. Like his four
brothers, he enlisted in the Confederate army.

He had a lot of company. According to some
sources, more than 90 percent of the young men
from Horry District wore the Confederate gray.
Horry District, unlike the Georgetown area, had
few slaves, so why did its young men march off to

war? The answer: Like most rank-and-file Confederate soldiers, they were fighting for Southern independence.

Less than 20 percent of white southerners owned slaves. Thinking southerners knew slavery was fated to end in America as it had recently ceased to exist in other western nations. The American anti-slavery movement had been strong in the South until the 1830s, and prominent southerners like George Washington and Robert E. Lee disliked slavery. Said Washington: "I am principled against this kind of traffic." Criticism from outspoken northern abolitionists, however, made many southerners defensive. They knew the New England shipping industry had supplied African slaves to the South, that northern states like Illinois and Indiana penalized and even banned black settlers, and that northerners had rioted against black residents in New York, Boston, Providence, and other cities. Southerners therefore considered northern condemnation of the South to be hypocritical and hateful. In 1859 the controversial John Brown, an abolitionist who had murdered slave owners in Kansas, seized the U.S. Arsenal at Harpers Ferry, Virginia, in a raid financed by northern abolitionists and designed to spark a southern slave revolt. Southerners were frightened by the raid and were offended when Brown was celebrated as a hero in the North.

The issue of slavery was explosive fuel tossed onto the smoldering fire of sectional differences and rivalry. The South was agricultural and rural; the North, urban and industrialized. Although they had much in common, southerners and northerners had different philosophies, different lifestyles, different goals. Southerners were generally suspicious of a centralized national government. They believed the vision of America's Founding Fathers had been subverted by northern politicians determined to erect a powerful federal government that, if unchecked, would someday, not only dominate the separate states, but would also rule the daily lives of individual citizens. With so little industry, southerners had to import most manufactured items—much of what was used in daily life—and they were incensed when northern congressmen enacted high tariffs on imported goods.

By 1860, southerners generally distrusted the northern business community and loathed northern politicians. They felt maligned, threatened, and despised by northern leaders. Confederate Gen. Isaac R. Trimble spoke for a generation of southerners when he issued these words to northern critics: "Our connection with you never had, from the early settlement of the colonies til now, any bond but that of political interest. Your bigotry & hatred of everything Southern drove us from you. . . . If she perishes, [the South] can go down to the grave of nations, with the proud boast that she has abundantly nourished with her blood the seeds of Liberty."

Led by South Carolina, which proclaimed itself independent in December 1860, eleven southern states seceded from the Union and formed the Confederate States of America. A wave of patriotism swept the South as southerners celebrated the creation of their new nation. They saw themselves as the new generation of Washingtons and Jeffersons, with northerners cast in the role of threatening outsiders much as the British had been viewed on the eve of the Revolution. They believed they had exercised their constitutional right of secession and were casting off the yoke of tyranny imposed by the federal government. Their new nation, southerners believed, reflected the vision of America's Founding Fathers far better than the union of the northern states. When Abraham Lincoln called for seventy-five thousand volunteers to invade the South and suppress "the insurrection," southerners were eager to defend their homes and protect their independence.

"A day of rejoicing it was," recalled a woman living near Georgetown. "It was now the time for every true man to study the interest of his country and to prepare for the many dangers staring him in the face . . . it is well to mention the spirit in which the cause was taken up." Talk of war dominated conversations, and southerners, like their counterparts in the north, believed the conflict would be brief, exciting, and bloodless. In Horry and Georgetown districts, young men from town and country rushed to join the army. Almost all inexperienced volunteers, they organized their own companies, elected officers, and selected company names. Among the volunteer units from the Grand Strand region who rushed to arms in the early burst of patriotism were the Horry Rough and Readys, the Georgetown Rifle Guards, the Lake Swamp Volunteers, the Bull Creek Guerrillas, the Brooks Rifle Guards, the Waccamaw Light Artillery, the Wachesaw Rifles, Marion's Men

When President Lincoln called for Northern volunteers to invade the South, young men from South Carolina and other southern states rushed to join the Confederate army.

(Library of Congress)

of Winyah, the Horry Hussars, the Wee Nee Volunteers, and the Horry Dixie Boys.

A veteran from the early days of the war remembered the scene years later as a boisterous, riotous event of great ambition and greater confusion. One company "reported in such disorganization," he recalled, "that the colonel declined to receive it and it returned home."

The eager troops marched up and down the local parade grounds, serenaded by regimental bands, trailed by pet dogs, and cheered by wives and sweethearts. "We joyed in the valor of our little state," remembered a South Carolina woman years

On the home front in Horry County and elsewhere in Dixie, southern women supported their men at war and learned to endure hard times.

(South Carolina Confederate Relic Room and Museum)

later. "Without understanding it at all, we had unconsciously imbibed state sovereignty from our very cradles. Without one misgiving or premonition of coming evil we entered the four years of war. . . . All was bright and hopeful that first year as we saw fathers, brothers and friends don the gray and march away, thinking they would soon be back and all would be well."

The reality of war struck hard in July 1861, when casualty lists were posted from the battle of First Manassas. Although the carnage of First Manassas would be dwarfed by the bloodbath to come, at the time it was the largest battle ever fought on the North American continent, with almost sixty thousand troops involved and a toll of almost five thousand casualties. "A bitter cry went up," recalled a South Carolina mother. "Lamentation, weeping and mourning for the sons that were not. That cry was not to be stilled for four long years and oh, the sadness, the pity of it! In those four years there were but few homes in our community to which there came not the fearful tidings of a loved one killed, wounded, captured or missing. The women lived on the mails and gathered round the bulletin boards to read the latest news from the front."

As an agricultural society, the South could not develop the industrial capacity and economic system needed to wage sustained warfare. Confederate leaders believed the war would be brief and that southern cotton would pay off all debts, so the Confederate government printed massive amounts of paper money backed by little more than high hopes. Inflation exploded throughout the South and affected everyone, including residents of the Grand Strand area. By 1864, it took $46 to buy what $1 had bought in 1861. By spring of 1865, articles that had cost $1 four years earlier were selling for $90. A bar of soap cost $3. An iron post was $100. A bottle of apple brandy could fetch $70. Basic commodities disappeared. Something as common as a sewing needle became a carefully protected treasure. Life was hard, but like southern women everywhere, the women of the Grand Strand region learned to cope with hardship.

A Horry woman who endured the war years as a teenager recalled:

> We learned to weave, spin and knit—to do many things during the war, for there was no way to get anything—it had to be made. We did this cheerfully. My mother had two nice dresses bought before the war, these she gave to us, telling us that we could remodel them and they could be our best dresses.
>
> [To make] homespun dresses . . . father bought [cotton] from the wagons from Fayetteville, which came through the county selling black cotton for weaving. We did not know how to put it in the loom, but Mother knew. She set up the looms for us and we wove the cloth to make our dresses. These were made with a blouse waist and plain skirt, with trimmed collars and cuffs. We had no button molds, so we cut pasteboard molds and covered them with black silk, then sewed on black jet beads. Now that our dresses were finished, we must have hats. These were made of strips of palmetto. Palmetto braids were made by stripping the palmetto into small strips and braiding them into hats. The braids were very smooth and white. We could buy palmettos in

Horry County homemakers, like these southern women, formed sewing societies to knit socks and make uniforms for the men who had gone to war. *(Library of Congress)*

Conway at ten cents a bunch. Two bunches would make each of us a sailor hat.

Recipes substituted innovation for hard-to-find ingredients. Apple pie without apples was made by adding butter, nutmeg, and sweetener to a bowl of wet crackers. Parched acorns roasted with a dab of bacon fat became coffee. Home remedies replaced store-bought medicines. Table salt boiled in vinegar was touted as a cure for dysentery. A mixture of milk, pulverized charcoal, and turpentine was dispensed to treat diphtheria and scarlet fever. A troublesome cough would be silenced by a dose of vinegar and laudanum.

In the rice region of Georgetown District, women on the homefront were left to manage sprawling plantations. Although many of the region's slaves left home to join a huge contraband community of escaped slaves on Winyah Bay's North Island, most servants chose to remain loyal to their owners and keep life going as much like normal as possible. In Horry District, however, most residents were more like typical southerners and lived on small farms without any slave labor. Left alone with only the children and the elderly, the women there struggled to manage the farm and family alone—while worrying about the menfolk off at war. Life had always been demanding in rural Horry, and the war only made it harder.

A glimpse of Horry's hardscrabble lifestyle was preserved by an observant English housekeeper, Elizabeth Collins, who came to Conwayboro in 1862 while employed by Georgetown rice planter Plowden C. J. Weston:

> At an early hour of a very fine day, Prince drove us to Conwayboro, a distance of 40 miles, through a rough country full of stumps and trees and roads of very deep sand. After driving about 18 miles, it was necessary to rest the horses and take a little refreshment. Having a few hours before met a kind old country farmer who invited Mrs. Weston to call on his old woman, we went there. On our arrival at the farm house, we were welcomed by the farmer's wife and a host of dogs, one looking as pleased as the other. In less than half an hour a smoking dish of sweet potatoes was brought in. They did not in any way look tempting, but I could not refuse the hospitality of the generous woman. Mrs. Weston having her little pet dog with her who was very fond of sweet potatoes, we managed to eat two.

Local women also had to endure the threat of enemy invasion. Federal warships probed the area's inlets and rivers, and naval landing parties occasionally raided riverside plantations, destroying buildings, seizing livestock, and stealing personal property. In Horry District, an outlaw band of Confederate deserters and draft dodgers took advantage of the absence of military-age men and terrorized residents with raids on local farms and homes. They met their match, however, when they raided a farm in the Cool Spring community. It was defended by a young Horry woman named Ellen Cooper, her sister, and C. L. Johnson, an incapacitated Confederate soldier who was home mending a battle wound. Extracts from Ellen Cooper's memoir record the raid:

> My sister and I had our pistols in hand. Mr. Johnson was on the porch, rifle and cartridge box beside him. It was a dark, rainy night. Then the rifle shot! Sister and I fell to the floor and crawled inside the room. The raiders returned the fire again and again. I got up, hoping I might shoot and hit some of them before they forced entry. I stood there a few minutes when I saw the flare from a rifle and heard the crash of a ball as it went through the shingles in the top of the house above my head. I stood there and fired back as near as I could to the place that I thought they were. Again they shot back. I shot again, dropped quickly to the floor and crawled into the room. I heard Mr. Johnson returning their fire. Now all became quiet.
>
> The next day Capt. Ervin of the home guard came with his company to Cool Spring and searched the woods. They brought in one of the deserters they had

Alarmed by Northern naval raids, some coastal residents fled inland, seeking—like these southern refugees—to escape the threat of Northern forces. *(Library of Congress)*

captured. He was tied to a tree in the yard and told that the law for deserters from the army was death. He begged them to spare his life and he would tell them the names of all the men in the raid and where to find the things that had been taken away.

He gave the names of those who were in the raid. Some of them had been wounded. One of them was shot and killed on the farther side of the river near the foot of the [Waccamaw River bridge in Conway] and another was killed at Board Landing. After this the raiding stopped.

In 1865, after four years of suffering on the southern homefront, the war ended, but the hardships did not. South Carolina's economy was wrecked, schools and businesses had been disrupted or destroyed; the state capital and a swath of small towns across the state lay in ruins from William Tecumseh Sherman's march to the sea. For the small farmers who populated Horry District, life would be even harder. With determination and an independent spirit, however, survivors came home from camp and battlefield and tried to resume normal lifestyles. Others would never return. Their bodies lay in soldiers' graves beneath distant, bloody ground in places like Virginia and Tennessee.

One who did return was Pvt. Hilliard Todd. He had endured numerous battles and survived several wounds to return home to Conwayboro. He alone among five brothers survived the war.

Generations of southerners, including residents of the Grand Strand region, would arise and pass before the heartache, hardships, and sacrifice of the War Between the States would dissolve from memory into history.

Bands of deserters and draft dodgers robbed and raided civilians in isolated areas of the South, like Horry County.

CHAPTER • ELEVEN

THE
ADMIRAL'S
SURPRISE

ADM. JOHN DAHLGREN WAS A BROAD-shouldered, fierce-looking man who carried himself with proper posture and sported a carefully maintained handlebar mustache. As commander of the Federal navy's South Atlantic Blockading Squadron, his job was to blockade the South Carolina coast during the War Between the States, including the region now known as the Grand Strand.

He admired its beauty, but the strip of coastline from Little River to Winyah Bay was a constant source of irritation to him, and Dahlgren was determined to punish the Confederates who protected the region and caused him frustration and anger.

This day, however, 1 March 1865, Admiral Dahlgren had reason to be cheerful. He had finally captured the port of Georgetown, which would bring an end to the problem of the Grand Strand. Georgetown was the headquarters for the Confederate forces in the area, and now, after four years of war, the port was finally occupied by Northern marines and Dahlgren's warships. His invasion of Winyah Bay had succeeded without loss of lives or ships. Georgetown officials had surrendered their town, and Dahlgren's sailors now occupied Battery White, the huge Confederate fort on the bay. The invasion had been postponed almost two years because Battery White was such a strong fortification, but when Northern warships arrived to bombard the fort, its Southern defenders were gone.

Earlier on the morning of March 1, Dahlgren had toured the sprawling earthen fort, looking at its big guns and admiring the surrounding live oaks. Now aboard his flagship, the USS *Harvest Moon*, Dahlgren sat down at his stateroom desk as the ship steamed across Winyah Bay. He picked up a pen, dipped it into an inkwell, and began to write an official report on the taking of Georgetown and the closing of the bothersome Grand Strand area.

The secretary of the navy, Gideon Welles, would be pleased to learn of Georgetown's capture. Since the beginning of the war, he had wanted the navy to seize Georgetown and close the many inlets of the Grand Strand, but subduing the region had been difficult. Early in the war Federal warships began blockading the Southern coast, trying to stop

Confederate soldiers were deployed to protect coastal areas like the Grand Strand, but fewer troops were available for coastal defense as the war dragged on. *(National Archives)*

the Confederacy from exchanging cotton and other products for war materials from England.

The navy had successfully blockaded Charleston, but the long strip of coast from Little River to Winyah Bay contained too many small inlets and creeks for the Northern warships to patrol. On dark, moonless nights, gray blockade runners fueled by smokeless coal would slip quietly out of places like Murrells Inlet. They would hug the darkened coastline for a few miles, then turn seaward and slip unseen between the distant Federal blockaders.

The traffic from Georgetown, Murrells Inlet, and Little River was minor compared to a major Southern port like Wilmington, but by February

1865 Wilmington and all other major Southern ports had been closed by Northern forces, and supplies coming from the smaller ports had become increasingly important. From the Grand Strand inlets blockade-runners took cargoes of turpentine, cotton, or rice to Nassau or Bermuda and then on to England, where they were exchanged for weapons, military equipment, medicine, or food vital to the embattled South.

The Lincoln administration wanted the blockade-runners stopped, and it had fallen to Admiral Dahlgren to perform the task. For a while the Federal navy had easy control of the Grand Strand. The earthen forts built by the Confederates around Winyah Bay at the beginning of the war were abandoned when their garrisons were shipped off to fight in Virginia and Tennessee. Northern warships then probed the region's inlets and steamed up the rivers emptying into the bay. Landing parties destroyed salt-making stations and plundered riverside plantations.

In May 1862, for instance, the USS *Albatross* steamed into Winyah Bay, turned into the Sampit River, and cruised along the Georgetown waterfront with its cannon trained on the port's buildings. Frightened residents watched with growing concern as the warship steamed upriver, turned around, then cruised past the town again.

As the *Albatross* passed the Georgetown docks the second time, a brazen Georgetown woman appeared in the bell tower of the town hall and defiantly unfurled a large Confederate flag. The captain of the warship, Comdr. George Prentiss, could easily have removed the flag and the flag waver with a blast of cannon fire. He declined, however, to commit an act unbecoming an officer and a gentleman and took the *Albatross* back to sea.

Such displays of Northern naval power alarmed the affluent rice planters of the region, who persuaded the Confederate government in 1863 to erect Battery White to protect the area. The huge fort was built overlooking the bay at Mayrant's Bluff below Georgetown, and the enemy naval raids were dramatically reduced.

By the time Admiral Dahlgren assumed command of the squadron off South Carolina, Battery White presented a formidable appearance. Dahlgren wanted to assault the fort, but the forces needed to attack such a strong post could not be spared from the major ports under blockade.

Dahlgren instead concentrated on ending the blockade-running traffic from Murrells Inlet and Little River. He especially disliked Murrells Inlet, which produced most of the traffic north of Georgetown. Some of the products slipping out of there somehow appeared on the shelves of Northern merchants, which infuriated the secretary of the navy. He ordered Dahlgren to bottle up Murrells Inlet, but it was an order Dahlgren found difficult to execute.

In April 1863 he sent two warships into the inlet on a raid. They burned the English blockade-runner *Golden Liner* and shelled four other ships. A month later another raid destroyed one blockade-runner, sank four others, and destroyed one hundred bales of cotton awaiting shipment. Despite the raids,

Speedy Southern blockade runners tried to elude Northern warships and supply the Confederacy with vital war materiel and needed consumer goods.

however, ships continued to sneak in and out of Murrells Inlet. Adding to Dahlgren's frustration, several landing parties were surprised and captured by Confederate cavalry in the area.

In retaliation Dahlgren decided to invade Murrells Inlet. A few days after Christmas 1863, he dispatched six warships—the *Nipsic, Sanford, Daffodil, Geranium, Ethan Allen,* and *George Mangham*—with a force of 250 marines. They were ordered to launch a surprise dawn attack on Murrells Inlet, kill or capture all Southern troops, and destroy everything within reach.

The six-ship flotilla anchored off the inlet on the night of 31 December 1863, and the commanding officers coordinated their attack plans. At first light the ships would steam into the inlet, bombard the shore with cannon fire, then put the marines ashore for battle. Fortunately for the residents of Murrells Inlet, a winter gale struck the area during the night, and the invasion was canceled—perhaps because the troops were seasick.

Not until February 1865 did Dahlgren receive permission to launch a serious attack on the area. That month, after the Confederates evacuated Charleston, he was given a full battalion of marines and sailors to use against Georgetown, which had become one of the few Atlantic ports still held by the Confederacy. The assault force was supported by three heavily armed warships, the *Pawnee, Mingoe,* and *Nipsic.* Troops would be landed on the Santee River below Winyah Bay, then would march up South Island Road and attack Battery White from the rear. As the troops prepared for their assault, however, the *Mingoe* picked up some deserters from Battery White who reported that all Southern troops had been moved inland to oppose Sherman's army, leaving Battery White abandoned.

The three warships entered Winyah Bay, and the lead vessel, the *Mingoe,* fired four rounds into Battery White, whose deserted guns remained silent. A detachment of marines was posted in the abandoned fort, and soon afterward Dahlgren sent the *Mingoe* and the *Catalpa* upstream to demand Georgetown's surrender.

The warships anchored with guns trained on the Georgetown waterfront, while a landing party went ashore. Led by Ens. Allen Noyes, the Northern seamen entered the town hall and demanded

Georgetown's surrender. City officials reluctantly turned over the keys to the town hall. Noyes sent three sailors up into the building's bell tower, where they raised the U.S. flag. It was Friday, 24 February 1865.

Four days later Admiral Dahlgren arrived in Georgetown aboard the *Harvest Moon*. He reviewed his troops in a ceremony on Georgetown's Front Street. Then he officially declared the region to be under martial law. When finished, the admiral triumphantly returned to the *Harvest Moon* and steamed downstream to Battery White. He spent the night of 28 February anchored off the captured fort, walked along its walls the next morning, then returned to his flagship for the voyage back to his squadron.

Sitting contentedly at his stateroom desk as the *Harvest Moon* steamed away from Battery White, Dahlgren wrote a glowing report to the secretary of the navy, boasting of the capture of the fort and the occupation of Georgetown. Finally, the nettlesome Grand Strand had been brought into submission. No longer would Dahlgren have to endure embarrassment because of the region's impudent defenders. Never again would he have to send the secretary those humiliating reports of captured seamen and escaped blockade-runners. He had finally brought the region under his thumb.

At that moment an explosion shook the *Harvest Moon* and shattered the wall of Dahlgren's stateroom, almost knocking the admiral out of his chair. The flagship had hit a homemade mine, built and launched by a local citizen. The explosion blew a

Adm. John Dahlgren brought the power of the U.S.
Navy against the blockade runners operating out of
Grand Strand–area inlets. *(National Archives)*

huge hole in the vessel's hull, and within five minutes the *Harvest Moon* sank to the bottom of Winyah Bay.

Admiral Dahlgren escaped with nothing but the uniform he wore and the ship's logbook. He had encountered a single act of resistance—and it had cost him his flagship in the waters of the South Carolina Grand Strand. Now he would have to write one more report to the secretary of the navy.

Dahlgren's flagship, the USS *Harvest Moon*, became a casualty of his attack on Georgetown's defenses.

CHAPTER TWELVE

UNCLE JUMBO AND THE MALLARDS

THEY CAME IN GREAT CLOUDS THAT SEEMED to blacken the winter sun. By the thousands they descended on Winyah Bay, and the rush of their wings caused a great roar. They were mallards, beautiful green-headed ducks from Canada's frozen lakes. Every winter they came south to the warmer waters of the Grand Strand.

They came because of the rice fields that lay abandoned by the end of the nineteenth century. By then even the die-hard planters were giving up hope of recapturing the pride and profits of the old rice empire. The empire was gone, but the rice fields remained, creating one of the richest hunting grounds in the world. Not in Europe, nor in China, nor in Canada were so many ducks found in one place. In the 1890s America's best-known hunter came to the Grand Strand in search of mallards, and because of him rich men once again walked the old plantations.

He was the son of a Presbyterian minister. His father had never earned more than six hundred dollars a year and had died early, leaving the son at the age of sixteen to care for the family. The young man worked hard, first as a grocery clerk, then as an aide in an institution for the blind, and finally as a public official. He finished law school and worked his way to the top—district attorney, sheriff, mayor, governor, and finally, president of the United States. His name was Grover Cleveland, and in 1894 he came to the Grand Strand to hunt ducks.

As mayor of Buffalo, Cleveland had become famous for trying to end corruption in city government. His reforms were so popular he was elected governor of New York before his term as mayor ended. He became a hero for his crackdown on corruption in state government, and before his term as governor ended, he was elected president.

The presidential campaign was a mudslinger. He became the first Democratic president since the Civil War, and the opposition dug deep to produce a scandal: an illegitimate son fathered when Cleveland was young. "Ma, ma, where's my pa?" the opposition chanted. "Gone to the White House! Ha, ha, ha!" Pressed by his party to lie about his sin, Cleveland refused. "It is true," he said and vowed to overcome his past.

In the 1890s Winyah Bay was considered one of the best duck hunting regions in North America.

He won the White House, but his political reforms so angered his party that he received scant support for re-election and was defeated by Republican Benjamin Harrison after one term. "Take good care of the furnishings," Mrs. Cleveland reportedly told the White House staff. "We'll be back in four years." He did return, narrowly beating incumbent Harrison to become the only American president elected to split terms.

In his second term Cleveland struggled to rid the federal government of the political corruption of the era. He was unsuccessful, but Americans loved him for trying. Most southerners revered him because he tried to heal the wounds of the Civil War. Once, he ordered all captured Confederate battle flags returned to the southern states. Opposition by Union veterans forced him to rescind the order, but southerners were heartened by the effort.

In the fall of 1894, early in his second term, Cleveland planned a hunting trip in the south. To escape the White House, he loved nothing better than the solitude of a duck blind. He had hunted near North Carolina's Outer Banks a year before, and now he wanted to go somewhere else. A friend of his, Edward Porter Alexander, a former Confederate general, owned South Island on Winyah Bay near Georgetown. Alexander knew that the duck hunting in his area was unsurpassed, and he dazzled the president with his description of the region. This year, Cleveland declared, he would go to Winyah Bay.

At 6:10 A.M. on 17 December 1894 the president's train rolled into Georgetown. Cleveland was quickly escorted from the train to the *Wisteria*, a lighthouse tender, which anchored near Muddy Bay, a section of Winyah Bay known for its duck shooting. Early next morning Cleveland enjoyed his first day in the rice fields. Dressed in a brown corduroy hunting suit and wearing hip boots, he was taken to a stand in the marshes by Sawney Caines, a young Georgetown hunting guide. Caines was raised along the rice fields, and his father had once set a record by dropping 166 ducks in succession without missing.

The president's party felled forty-nine ducks on their first shoot. Cleveland was the group's best shot and dropped twenty-nine of the birds. Such a harvest of game was common in 1894, when local hunters would sometimes bag more than two hundred ducks in one day's shooting.

Back on the *Wisteria* Cleveland tended only to the unavoidable presidential chores, reading mail and dispatches that arrived daily by train from Washington. He did not want the presidency to interfere with his Christmas vacation. "I don't want to see a newspaper while I'm here," he told his aides. When a reporter from Charleston's *News and Courier* appeared in a tugboat alongside the *Wisteria*, he was politely dismissed. Cleveland's aides also turned down a boatload of Georgetown dignitaries who came to invite the president to a reception. The disappointed officials left glum faced but cheered up when the president sent word he would attend their celebration.

The second day of Cleveland's hunt dawned perfect for duck shooting: The temperature was below freezing, and a brisk wind blew from the north. The president downed thirty ducks that day, but he left more in the marsh than empty shell cartridges. Guided to a marshy spot later known as "the president's stand," he made the mistake of trying to walk through the marsh mud. Cleveland was a big man—his nickname was Uncle Jumbo—and as he tried to cross the marsh he became mired in the dark goo. Inexperienced at walking through marshland, he tried to lift one foot, then the other, and found he could not move. He struggled. He strained. He pulled his legs with all his strength. Nothing helped. Held fast by his huge weight and the suction of

President Grover Cleveland, also known as
Uncle Jumbo, was a beloved figure in the South,
where he loved to go duck hunting.
(Library of Congress)

marsh mud, he only sank deeper. He had struggled
until breathless when Sawney Caines found him.

The young guide almost panicked. Here was the
president of the United States out of breath, stuck in
the mud, and sinking deeper into the marsh of
Winyah Bay. Caines tugged at the president's legs
and pulled the big man's arms, but nothing would
budge him. Finally, in desperation Caines mustered

phenomenal strength and jerked the president out of his boots. Once Cleveland was free, Caines could not put the president of the United States back in the marsh in his stocking feet, so he carried the huge man to the *Wisteria* on his shoulders, stepping skillfully through the marsh mud too quickly to bog down.

After five days of duck shooting, Grover Cleveland put aside his hunting clothes and donned a dark suit for his trip back to Washington. Winyah Bay had lived up to its reputation. On the afternoon of 22 December Cleveland left his hunting spot and returned to Georgetown on the *Wisteria*. As the ship docked at the town wharf, the president was met by a wild and colorful celebration. The port's steamboats, tugboats, and schooners were gaily decorated with red, white, and blue bunting. So were the streets, stores, and homes of Georgetown. As Cleveland stepped off the ship, church bells rang, the tugboats and lumber mills blew their steam whistles, and the region's residents shouted repeated hurrahs.

A procession of horse-drawn carriages took the president through streets lined with hundreds of citizens. Folks from surrounding farms, businessmen in derby hats, farmers in bib overalls, and swamp dwellers in coonskin caps stood along the parade route and cheered as Cleveland passed. He was escorted to Winyah Indigo Society Hall, which was decorated with palmetto fronds, Spanish moss, and colorful flags. There he dined on a feast prepared by area women, then stood to make a brief speech.

"I leave your state," he told the hushed audience, "where I have gained in health and strength, to take up again the troublesome, irksome state duties with the kindest and most grateful remembrances. When this outing is but a memory, this occasion will stand out clearly—the memory of the welcome and Godspeed of Georgetown."

After toasts by city officials, Cleveland was soon aboard the presidential train, chugging north to Washington. Along with the president and his entourage, the train carried a hamper of dressed ducks for the president to dispense to favored friends and cabinet members.

Back in Georgetown, meanwhile, city officials began to experience a peculiar turn of events. From throughout the nation letters began arriving—all requesting information about duck hunting and hotel accommodations. Cleveland's hunt had been reported daily by major newspapers, and thousands of enthusiastic sportsmen had read the accounts of the hunters' paradise in South Carolina.

Soon wealthy sportsmen from New York, New Jersey, Pennsylvania, and Chicago began appearing in Georgetown, drawn by newspaper reports of Grover Cleveland's great hunt. It was an age when the industry and business of the north were producing men of great wealth. Many of those who came to hunt in the region became enchanted by the beauty and wildlife of the area. They found they could buy the old rice plantations along the region's rivers for a fraction of what they spent on New York City townhouses and European chateaux. Those who bought plantations attracted others. One by one the old plantations were occupied by rich northerners.

Expert shots like these Georgetown-area hunters could down
hundreds of ducks in a single morning.
(Belle W. Baruch Foundation)

Natives of the area jokingly called it "the second
Yankee invasion," but they were grateful for the
economic and social contributions made by the
newcomers. After decades of neglect, the rice plantations once again housed wealthy and influential
owners. The new plantation masters knew nothing of rice, but they made a distinctive impact on
the Grand Strand. Families like the Huntingtons,
the Kimbels, the Vanderbilts, and the Yawkeys

influenced education, developed the business community, improved communications, fostered appreciation for the arts, preserved the environment, and
encouraged development—just like the plantation
owners of an earlier era.

And it all happened because Uncle Jumbo liked
to hunt mallards.

CHAPTER • THIRTEEN

THE

KILLER HURRICANE

OF 1893

FAR OUT TO SEA THE GREAT DEADLY MON-
ster moved toward shore. It blackened the sky and
sucked the ocean into colossal waves. It howled
and roared, blowing rain and ocean spray like an
angry, frenzied demon.

It was a powerful hurricane—one of the worst in
history—and in less than twenty-four hours, on 13
October 1893, it would strike drowsy Murrells Inlet
and Magnolia Beach. For years to come the great
storm would be recalled in awed terms and referred
to as the killer hurricane of 1893.

The day before the hurricane hit, fourteen-year-
old Jessamine Buck stood on the porch of her family's home at Murrells Inlet and looked toward the

ocean. Through the blowing rain she could see the family cottage on Magnolia Beach, eight miles across the marsh. For years her family had spent the summers at the cottage. They liked the beach so much their father had moved the family from their home on the Waccamaw River at Bucksport to the house at Murrells Inlet. They enjoyed living on the inlet with easy access to their beach cottage. The area had a special beauty, even in the rainy weather that had descended on the coast that week.

The rain worsened during the day, getting heavier shortly after Jessamine's mother and father left to go inland. They were scheduled to be back soon, and they left Jessamine and her brother, George, in the care of their older sister, Iola. It was too rainy to do anything outside, so the three of them stayed inside with the two family servants.

Across the marsh, on the other side of the creek from Murrells Inlet, Dr. Arthur Flagg and his wife Georgeanna were enjoying themselves despite the bad weather. Their children and grandchildren had come to the beach for a family reunion at the family's two beach cottages.

The beaches, inlets, and woodlands of the region were familiar to Dr. Flagg; his ancestors had lived on Waccamaw Neck since the colonial period. His grandfather, Henry Collins Flagg, a rice planter, had entertained President George Washington at Brookgreen Plantation in 1791, and his father, Ebenezer Flagg, had grown rice on Oak Lawn Plantation.

Like his father and grandfather, Arthur Flagg was a doctor. Now sixty-five years old, he could remember the era of the rice empire, which was still

Turn-of-the-century beach goers had no warning of
threatening weather. *(Horry County Museum CNB Collection)*

flourishing when he finished medical school and
came back to Waccamaw Neck. He married
Georgeanna Ward, the daughter of Joshua John
Ward, the richest planter in South Carolina. They
had seen the rice culture crumble after the Civil
War, but they remained on the Waccamaw, holding
on to their property when so many others gave up.
Like the Flaggs before him, Arthur had directed his
two sons to medical school, and now they were
doctors.

Both had joined their parents at Magnolia Beach,
the narrow spit of sand that would later be known
as Huntington Beach State Park. Arthur, Jr., had
brought his wife and five children and was also
accompanied by two sisters-in-law. They all stayed
in a cottage down the beach from his parents. The

other son, Ward, was staying in the cottage with his parents and had brought three of his nieces, Ann, Pauline, and Elizabeth Weston.

While the Flaggs swapped stories and laughed with the children, Cato Singleton and his wife were leaving the beach. Singleton was a middle-aged black man who had been born into slavery on a Waccamaw Neck plantation where the master followed the southern custom of naming slave children after classical figures like Caesar, Cupid, Nero, Neptune, Hercules, and Cato. He and his wife lived in the large black community on Waccamaw Neck and frequently drove their ox cart to Magnolia Beach.

They usually crossed the wide creek behind the beach at low tide when the oxen could easily wade through the marsh. This day Singleton was surprised when he came to the creek. The tide had not gone out as usual. The sandbars that normally protruded from the creek were under water, and the oyster beds were flooded. It was time for the tide to be going out, but instead it seemed to be coming in. It was almost dark, but Singleton could still see the marsh. Strangely, it was almost submerged.

The oxen barely made it across the creek, and on the land side of the marsh Singleton looked back at the ocean. What he saw made him shudder. The sky had darkened, but an eerie glow lit the sea. He hurriedly left. The strange light made him think of judgment and hell.

The rain became heavier after dark, and the wind began a low moan over the ocean. Foam blew off the whitecaps and the surf rose and fell on the beach with an unusual violence. Inside his parents' cottage, Ward Flagg began to worry. The gale season had begun early that year with a series of unusually severe storms. In June and August ferocious gales had struck the coast near Charleston, drowning hundreds.

Ward knew the coast had a history of deadly storms. In 1752 a hurricane rolled a seventeen-foot tidal wave over Charleston, drowning many residents and smashing five hundred buildings. The old-timers fearfully recalled the storm of 1822 that wiped out summer homes on Cedar Island south of Winyah Bay and was strong enough to wreck Georgetown's wooden courthouse. The worst storms came from the south and southeast, carried by the trade winds from the Caribbean. No one could accurately predict a storm in 1893, but Ward Flagg noted with mounting concern that the wind was blowing from the south.

No one in his cottage slept much that night. Soon after daybreak he braved the pelting rain to look at the ocean, and he did not like what he saw. The sea had advanced far beyond the high-tide mark, and with each wave it seemed a foot or two higher. The creek between the beach and the mainland had risen dramatically during the night, making evacuation impossible. They would have to wait out the storm on the beach. The cottages had survived a lot of gales, Ward told himself, and surely they could endure one more. If the area were flooded, they would just wait out the storm upstairs. No flood had ever gotten that high.

Across the swollen creek from the beach, Jessamine Buck and her brother George watched

Iola Buck

Jessamine Buck

George Buck

(Courtesy of Eugenia Buck Cutts)

the creek rise. The wind whipped huge waves on the inlet, rolling them ashore just like the ocean surf. After watching the rising water for a while, George decided to bring a neighbor, Mrs. Beaty, and her five children up to the Buck home from their house near the creek. The Buck house rested on high ground away from the marsh, but the Beaty home lay on low ground and was prone to flooding. He ran through the driving rain and brought Mrs. Beaty and her children back with him.

They had not been at the Buck house long when Mrs. Beaty told George she wanted to go back home for her children's nightclothes. George did not want her or anyone else to go back out in the storm, but Mrs. Beaty persisted. That afternoon he finally agreed to go, even though the gale had worsened. Mrs. Beaty sent her oldest daughter with him to help carry the clothes. The creek was now surging through the yard. But George thought they could wade through the water with little trouble.

Outside, the force of the wind almost knocked them down. They could barely hear and they were blinded by the stinging rain. Still, George bent his head and waded toward the Beaty house until Jessamine could see him no more through the rain.

On Magnolia Beach, Ward Flagg knew the family was in trouble. With each breaking wave the ocean spilled ten feet closer to the cottages. By early afternoon the surf covered the sand dunes and waves were breaking on the cottage walls. As a precaution, everyone moved upstairs. An hour later waves crashed through the downstairs windows and water began filling the first floor. Soon the full fury of the hurricane struck the cottage.

The structure began to shake and creak with the pull of the waves. The chimney toppled into the surf and boards began to come loose and float away. By mid-afternoon waves were breaking just under the second-story windows. Ward Flagg could feel the house beginning to come apart. He opened a back window and one-by-one members of the family climbed out the window, made their way across the porch roof, and climbed into a large cedar tree. Despite their ages, Arthur, Sr., and Georgeanna were able to traverse the roof and reach the tree. Perched on the roof, with the waves splashing their feet, were all the occupants of the cottage: Arthur, Sr., and Georgeanna; Ward Flagg; nieces Ann, Pauline, and Elizabeth; and the family servants.

As the waves rose higher, they watched the house break into sections, which were sucked out to sea. They climbed higher into the tree, but the surf rose with them until it was rolling waist high across their perches, and waves were crashing against their chests. Arthur, Sr., and Georgeanna began to weaken. A large wave pulled them loose, but Ward grabbed them before they were swept away.

Some of the servants were the first to drown, sucked away when they weakened. Ward grabbed a long-time servant named Mom Adeline when she lost her hold on a limb. "Hold on, Mom Adeline!" he shouted, but she could not, and she was swept away. One by one the other servants disappeared under the boiling waves. Two nieces also drowned, and he could do nothing to save them.

Georgeanna locked her arms around her husband's neck, while he held onto the tree. The waves pounded and pulled them, steadily eroding their strength. Finally, Georgeanna lost her grip and slipped beneath a wave. Arthur, Sr., immediately let go of the tree and embraced his wife as water swept over them. "Miss Georgie's gone!" he yelled to Ward. "I'm gone too!"

Ward saw his parents go beneath the surging waves, bob up once, and then disappear. He watched in helpless despair, unable to aid them. Holding onto the tree, he remembered his mother's frequent comment: "I wish I could die right with your father, and he would put his arms around me and we could go together." When Ward saw them last they were locked in an embrace.

Inside the Buck house at Murrells Inlet, Jessamine was desperate with fear. The ocean covered the distant beach and waist-deep waves were rolling through the yard, sweeping away chickens and breaking up the outbuildings. Terrified and afraid that George and the Beaty girl had drowned, Jessamine, Mrs. Beaty, and the servants carried the children outside and began wading inland. Buffeted by the wind and stunned by the force of the waves, they realized they would never make it. They turned around and fought their way back to the house just in time to see the front steps float away. The porch rose and fell with each wave and the foundation pillars began to crumble.

Jessamine and the others climbed back onto the bobbing porch just as George and the Beaty girl came around the corner of the house. Jessamine was overjoyed to see George alive, but the two had no time to celebrate. In the lower parts of the yard waves were now breaking in the limbs of the live oak trees. George knew the house would come apart or float off its pillars if he did not do something to stop it.

He swam out to a section of fence floating by and lashed it to the house in case a raft was needed. Then he climbed onto the porch, went inside the house, and knocked a hole in the parlor floor. He enlarged the hole with a saw, hoping the water would surge through the hole instead of lifting the house off its foundation. His plan worked: Water gushed through the hole and swept through the house, but the structure remained on its pillars.

From a perch atop some furniture, frightened Jessamine watched the family chickens float past the windows. Suddenly she realized the water was rushing in a different direction. The worst of the storm had passed, and the sea was flowing back toward the beach. The water rapidly retreated, draining from the house and the yard almost as quickly as it had come. An hour later, the rain ended and the sun beamed through the clouds. The Buck home was damaged and the yard was filled with debris, but they had all survived. Jessamine stood on the battered porch and looked across the flooded marsh toward the ocean. She could see Magnolia Beach again and the surf was breaking in its customary place, but something looked different. With a shock she realized the Flaggs' cottages were gone.

Only a few hours after his parents were swept away in the worst of the storm, Ward Flagg was able to climb down from the cedar tree. Except for his niece, Ann, and two servants, he was alone. Almost everyone in his cottage had drowned, and most of the occupants of his brother's cottage were gone too. The death count on Magnolia Beach totaled nineteen.

Days after the hurricane passed, volunteers continued searching for bodies, while others removed debris. Carcasses of cows, horses, and other livestock were left hanging in trees. Wreckage was strewn everywhere. The bodies of the Flaggs and their servants were recovered far from the cottages. Some were found in the marsh creek. Others washed ashore miles from Magnolia Beach. The body of Arthur, Sr., was discovered in the marsh, covered with mud. He still wore the vest he had put on the morning of the storm, and in his pocket his watch still ticked. Weeks passed before the succession of funerals ended. Finally, at nearby All Saints Church, the last victim of the killer hurricane of 1893 was buried beneath the live oaks and Spanish moss. Across Waccamaw Neck, on Magnolia Beach, the surf foamed peacefully on the sand.

CHAPTER • FOURTEEN

FDR's
SECRET
VISIT

ON EASTER SUNDAY 1944 A MOTORCADE OF
armed guards drove through Georgetown, crossed
the muddy Waccamaw, and turned into the wilderness of Hobcaw Barony. As the cars bumped along
the sandy lane toward their destination, President
Franklin D. Roosevelt looked out the window of his
vehicle at the forest of Carolina pine and began to
relax.

Roosevelt was gravely ill, with less than a year to
live. Dark circles surrounded his eyes. His face had
an unhealthy grayish cast. His hands trembled constantly, and the slightest exercise left him breathless. For twenty-three years he had been unable to

walk because of the polio that paralyzed his legs in 1921, at the age of thirty-nine. Now he moved everywhere by wheelchair. He had crutches, but he seldom used them. Aides carried him when necessary, but he normally sped through the White House in a special wheelchair, with his aides jogging alongside.

He had not beaten polio but had kept it from beating him. After serving as state senator, he was, despite the handicap, elected governor of New York and, in 1932, the nation's president. What he faced now, however, was more dangerous than paralysis. For seven years he had suffered hypertension. His arteries were hardening, and he was slowly dying of congestive heart failure. With the best of care, his heart specialist knew, Roosevelt might live one more year.

He never asked the doctors for details, and they did not offer any. He had other subjects on his mind. In Europe Hitler's legions were being driven across Poland by the Soviet army. Berlin smoldered from Allied bombing. Italy had collapsed under an Allied invasion. General Dwight D. Eisenhower was counting down to D-Day and the long-awaited invasion of France. In the Pacific, General Douglas MacArthur and Admiral Chester Nimitz were driving the Japanese back toward their homeland, island by island, in a series of bloody encounters. In the desert of New Mexico and the hills of East Tennessee, American scientists were using money secretly provided by Roosevelt to build the first atomic bomb.

FDR was now in his third term. The pressures of office and the demands of war had further drained

In 1944 President Franklin D. Roosevelt appeared tired and unhealthy. *(FDR Library)*

his health. After a thorough physical, White House doctors told the president he needed two weeks in bed. Roosevelt lit one of the Camels he incessantly smoked, put it in his famous cigarette holder, held it at a jaunty angle, and ignored their advice as usual.

He did agree to take a vacation. He wanted to take a train to Miami, then fly to Guantanamo Bay in Cuba for a tropical holiday, but his doctors felt his condition was too poor for an airplane flight. Instead, he accepted Bernard Baruch's invitation to visit his Hobcaw Barony near Georgetown. Baruch had been a private adviser to several presidents, including Roosevelt, and several times he had encouraged FDR to visit Hobcaw. Many political leaders had been to Hobcaw, and the pleasures of visiting Baruch's barony were legendary in Washington.

Known as the Wizard of Wall Street, Baruch had become a millionaire in the stock market before he was thirty. By 1944 he was one of the richest men in the world. Most of his life had been spent in New York City, but he was a native of Camden, South Carolina. His father, a surgeon in the Confederate army, had moved the family to New York when Bernard was eleven. After his success on Wall Street, Baruch acquired a luxurious New York townhouse, a country estate, and a chateau in Europe. But his favorite place to visit was his native state.

"South Carolina is flesh of my flesh and bone of my bone," he would say. As a child he had vacationed at Pawley's Island, and he grew to love the Grand Strand. An enthusiastic hunter, he loved duck shooting on Winyah Bay. In 1907 he quietly began to buy the old rice plantations on the bay opposite Georgetown. By the time he completed his purchases, he had acquired 117,000 acres teeming with deer, wild hog, turkey, and quail, situated in a region renowned for duck hunting. After hearing his hunting stories, friends in New York and Washington would jokingly accuse Baruch of exaggerating—until they visited Hobcaw.

Baruch would normally stay at Hobcaw from Christmas until Easter, commuting to New York or Washington if necessary. At Hobcaw he entertained a parade of luminaries: senators, governors, bankers, businessmen, authors, actors, military leaders.

Winston Churchill and his daughter visited in 1932. Songwriter Irving Berlin came one year. So did authors H. G. Wells, Jack London, and Sherwood Anderson. Gen. Omar Bradley, *Time* magazine's Henry Luce, entertainer Billy Rose—all sampled Bernard Baruch's hospitality at Hobcaw.

Like Roosevelt they were enchanted with what they found: forests of pine, poplar, gum, and oak; cypress swamps, rice fields, marshlands; stands of palmetto and live oaks; ramshackle communities that had served as slave villages on the old plantations; and a long, deserted stretch of private beach.

On a bluff overlooking the bay, Baruch built a hunting lodge: a brick mansion with Georgian columns, surrounded by azaleas, camellias, and moss-trimmed oaks. Upstairs, the family bedrooms faced the bay, and the servants' quarters were at the rear. Downstairs, the hunting lodge had guest rooms, a large sitting room, a spacious dining room, a billiard room and library, and a giant kitchen for preparing wild game or lavish dinners. Hobcaw House offered almost every luxury available, including a servant whose sole job was to sweep attractive patterns in the sandy walkways outside. Missing, however, was a telephone. Baruch refused to install the instrument. Instead he accepted messages that were called into a general store in Georgetown, then ferried across the bay by boat.

Only when Roosevelt decided to visit did Baruch allow telephones to be temporarily installed in the house. Days before FDR arrived, a team of advance men transformed Baruch's retreat into a vacation White House. First, the Secret Service arrived to

Bernard Baruch, the Wall Street Wizard, was a native South Carolinian who had entertained countless dignitaries at his Grand Strand–area estate. *(FDR Library)*

"sanitize" the estate. They questioned servants, studied the nearby waterways, examined the house and stables, and prowled through the woodlands. Next, army signal corpsmen arrived. They put in two telephones for the president to use. One provided a direct link to the White House switchboard, and the other was used for private calls. Safety railing was erected on the dock in front of the house, and a flagpole was raised at the end of the little pier.

Roosevelt's trip to Hobcaw was top secret, but residents of the Grand Strand soon realized what was happening. White House correspondents from three wire services checked into Georgetown's Front Street Hotel. A Signal Corps railroad car loaded with communications equipment was pulled onto a Georgetown siding. Marines in combat camouflage patrolled the entrance to the estate, aided by a detachment of soldiers from Fort Jackson in Columbia. Coast Guard vessels cruised Winyah Bay. Secret Service agents armed with handguns and shotguns stood guard outside Hobcaw House, and Army Air Corps fighter planes made regular passes over the estate.

When Roosevelt's motorcade took him to Hobcaw House that Easter Sunday, he had one thing on his mind. "I want to sleep and sleep," he told Baruch. "Twelve hours every night." FDR would sleep late, eat breakfast about nine o'clock, then undergo a brief examination by his heart specialist. After another hour of rest, the president would examine the White House documents' pouch, which was flown down from Washington daily. At noon he would dictate letters for an hour, then eat a light lunch. Afternoons were left for fishing, sightseeing jaunts around Hobcaw, or more rest. After a casual dinner with Baruch and some White House advisers, Roosevelt could watch movies in a makeshift theater erected in one of the stables, but he seldom did. Instead, he would usually play a game of gin rummy or solitaire, or he would go to bed early.

He did little work at Hobcaw and entertained few visitors. Gen. Mark Clark arrived with a fresh report on the war in Europe, and First Lady Eleanor Roosevelt made a brief visit, accompanied by their daughter, Anna, the prime minister of Australia, and his wife. While FDR and the prime minister discussed the war in the Pacific, Mrs. Roosevelt learned to crab off the dock in front of the house.

After resting several days, Roosevelt allowed himself to be ferried into the creeks off Winyah Bay in the afternoon, sitting for hours in the April sun with a fishing pole. One day he took a deep-sea fishing trip off the Grand Strand, laughing at Baruch because the old sportsman was prone to seasickness. Other afternoons he chose to fish off the dock.

Roosevelt toured the old slave villages of Hobcaw and was driven down the dusty remnant of the old King's Highway. He learned about the British occupation of the area during the American Revolution, and he could see the rusting smokestack of Adm. John Dahlgren's flagship, sunk off Hobcaw during the Civil War. His favorite spot was Belle Isle Gardens, across the bay on the site of Battery White. The old Confederate fort had been converted into a private flower garden, which Roosevelt toured, admiring the blossoming azaleas and examining the old earthworks.

At Hobcaw, Roosevelt found the rest he needed so badly. "I like it here," he admitted. "I have been very comfortable down here. I want to come back. Down here I can do a little fishing and get lots of rest. I like it around Belle Isle Gardens—it is perfectly lovely."

Roosevelt enjoyed his vacation so much he extended it by two weeks, spending a full month at

Hobcaw Barony. Although one day of his vacation was spent enduring the discomfort of a gall bladder attack, most of his visit was uneventful—with the exception of one bizarre episode. Near the end of his vacation, while FDR slept peacefully in his suite, a Secret Service agent posted outside Hobcaw House encountered one of the numerous wild hogs that prowled the estate. Confronted by the snorting animal, the agent impulsively lowered his shotgun and pulled the trigger.

When the double-barreled shotgun boomed in the night, lights flashed on in Hobcaw House and alarmed Secret Service agents and soldiers ran outside, searching for a would-be assassin. Instead, they found the agent holding a smoking shotgun over a dead hog. The next morning FDR roared with laughter over the incident, but the hog-shooting agent was sent back to Washington on the next train.

In early May, when he could no longer postpone returning to Washington, Roosevelt summoned the three White House correspondents who had been waiting in Georgetown and held an informal news conference in the sitting room of Hobcaw House. He repeatedly brought the conference back to his vacation. "I have rested," he told the reporters. "Had a very quiet time. Been out in the sun as much as possible. Done some fishing. Some saltwater fishing in the mouth of the river, some off the inlet and some in the ponds. I would like to come down here again."

On Sunday, 7 May 1944, Roosevelt was again rolling down the halls of the White House. Aides commented on the change in his appearance. Color

When his doctors ordered him to rest in 1944, FDR relaxed at Hobcaw House, Bernard Baruch's spacious "hunting lodge."
(Belle W. Baruch Foundation)

had returned to his face, and the dark circles around his eyes were gone. His voice was firm, and his spirited, flip manner had returned. FDR's physician said the trip to Hobcaw had added months to Roosevelt's life.

Although improved, Roosevelt was living on borrowed time. Less than a year later, while vacationing at Warm Springs, Georgia, he would die of a cerebral hemorrhage. At the moment, however, he enjoyed his improved health. He resumed the demands of the Oval Office in a world at war, but even there he occasionally may have daydreamed about the fishing around Hobcaw.

CHAPTER FIFTEEN

THE
BIRTH OF
THE BEACH

WALKING ALONG THE BEACH WITH HIS
daughter, Franklin G. Burroughs could see what
others never imagined. To the east the Atlantic
stretched toward a long, straight horizon. To the
west he could see nothing but sand dunes, sea oats,
and myrtle bushes. Looking north and south, he
saw only deserted, secluded beach. Most people
thought the beachfront land was worthless, but
Franklin Burroughs knew better. He owned the
beachfront as far as he could see, and he owned the
myrtle bushes, scrub oaks, and pine forest for
almost fifteen miles inland.

"Someday," predicted Franklin G. Burroughs, "this whole strand will be a resort." *(Courtesy of Burroughs & Chapin Co., Inc.)*

In the 1890s the oceanfront interested few people. They could only see empty beach and pine barrens, but Franklin Burroughs could see the future. "I won't live to see it, and you may not," he told his daughter, "but someday this whole strand will be a resort."

Burroughs had come to the Grand Strand region from North Carolina some forty years before. Like other young and ambitious southerners of his day, he was heading west in search of a better life in Alabama, Arkansas, or Texas. En route he stopped to say good-bye to a cousin in Conway, a riverfront cluster of frame buildings marked by a brick court-house and jail. While in town he got a job as a clerk in a general store, and he never made it to the West. He had a businessman's savvy and quickly made a name for himself as a young man on the way up. He got a job constructing the town bridge, helped build the country gallows, then entered the naval stores industry. Tar, pitch, and turpentine from the region's pine forests were in great demand for use in constructing the wooden ships of the era. Industrious men could make a fortune shipping the resin products to New England shipbuilders.

His business ventures were interrupted by the War Between the States. At the beginning of the war he joined the Brooks Rifle Guards from Horry County and remained with his unit when it was merged into Confederate service as a company of the Tenth South Carolina Infantry. He survived some of the bloodiest fighting of the war in the Confederate Army of Tennessee only to be captured and confined as a prisoner of war at Camp Douglas, the notorious Federal prison camp near Chicago. He endured the hardship of prison life with stubborn determination and returned to his business in Conway at the end of the war.

During the grim years of Reconstruction, he entered a partnership with another former

Confederate, Benjamin G. Collins, and the two created the Burroughs and Collins Company. Together they built their business into what some people claimed was the largest producer of naval stores in the country. They used their profits to build a local empire of mercantile stores, lumber mills, turpentine production, and steamboats.

By then Franklin was an old man. During his lifetime the Burroughs and Collins Company had acquired thousands of acres of woodlands for timber production, including much of the long, wide beach between Little River and Murrells Inlet. The coastline curved sharply westward to create a wide beach with gentle currents, called Long Bay by the local residents. Franklin Burroughs knew that beachfront resorts like Coney Island were reaping great fortunes up north, and he believed the same thing could happen someday on Long Bay.

Already people from as far away as Florence, more than seventy miles from the beach, were riding a new railway to Conway, where they would board steamboats to Wachesaw or Grahamville on the Waccamaw. From there they would ride wagons or ox carts to the beach, where they would pitch tents and play in the surf. Why not build a connecting railroad across company property, Burroughs reasoned, laying track from Conway to the beach fifteen miles away? It could serve the timber crews working east of Conway, and it could open the beach to more visitors. They could ride the Burroughs and Collins railroad, stay in a company hotel, and maybe even buy some real estate from the firm.

In 1899 the Burroughs and Collins Company began building the railroad Burroughs envisioned. It was called the Conway, Coast and Western Railroad. Rail by rail and spike by spike it inched toward the beach. In 1900 it was finished and the line opened for service. A secondhand locomotive named Black Maria was coupled to two old passenger cars and began chugging back and forth between Conway and the beach, hauling passengers to the new resort, which most folks called New Town.

It was a demanding ride. Black Maria was an aging steam engine formerly used to pull logs from North Carolina swamps. The best passenger cars owned by the railroad were discarded relics once used on New York City's elevated tramway. By the time the passengers arrived at the beach, their faces might be blackened by soot and their clothes burned by embers blown from the engine's smokestack.

In 1901, soon after the beach railroad opened, the Burroughs and Collins Company built a beach hotel called Sea Side Inn. Nearby were a pavilion and a bathhouse. The company sponsored a contest among the guests and workers at the hotel to pick an official name for the new resort. Although Edgewater was a popular choice, the winning name was Myrtle Beach, picked because of the wax myrtle that grew wild along the strand.

Summer weekends began to attract increasing numbers of visitors. Attired in ankle-length bathing suits of mattress ticking, female beachgoers splashed in the surf with husbands and boyfriends, who usually swam in old clothes. After a dip in the

Surrounded by myrtle bushes and sand dunes, Sea Side Inn—the first hotel in Myrtle Beach—stood ready for guests at the turn of the century. *(Horry County Museum)*

ocean, vacationers could take a shower in the bathhouse. Atop each shower stall was a rain barrel from which water ran through a hose into the stall. After supper at Sea Side Inn, guests could take a romantic walk on the beach or dance to fiddle music in the pavilion.

Many vacationers liked new Myrtle Beach well enough to buy property. Oceanfront lots sold for twenty-five dollars apiece in 1910. Vacationers who could afford to build cottages costing five hundred dollars received an extra lot free as an incentive toward quality development of the resort.

In 1912 Simeon B. Chapin stepped off the train in Conway, and before he got back aboard he had forever affected the future of the fledgling resort. Chapin was a Chicago businessman who owned vacation homes on Wisconsin's Lake Geneva, in New York City, and at Pinehurst, North Carolina. He had been introduced to Burroughs and Collins

Company officials by a Pinehurst real estate dealer who knew the company was looking for an investor to help develop Myrtle Beach. Chapin was intrigued by the potential of the new resort, but he had decided Myrtle Beach was too far from Chicago to interest him. He had come to Conway to personally deliver his refusal to the officials of Burroughs and Collins.

The company was headquartered in a modest frame building on Conway's Main Street. Chapin met with the company leaders and explained his decision not to invest in Myrtle Beach. They were disappointed, but they thanked him anyway and graciously said good-byes. A few minutes after leaving, Chapin reappeared at the open door and asked if anyone would be interested in a full partnership. Company officials happily agreed and shook hands on the deal. The new partnership was called Myrtle Beach Farms. It would deal in farming and timber production, but its chief aim would be the development of Myrtle Beach into a major resort.

Ten years later Myrtle Beach had grown into a modest but promising resort. It sported new guest houses, a new pavilion, a fishing pier, and a slowly expanding line of beach cottages. Its potential was showing, and in 1925 a wealthy visionary appeared with a grand design.

John T. Woodside was a millionaire textile executive from Greenville, South Carolina, and his cotton mill was reported to be the largest in the world. Those who knew him said he was backed by unlimited finances. Woodside had a vision of transforming little Myrtle Beach into a glamorous oceanside playground for the nation's rich, who seemed to be in constant search of recreation in the Roaring Twenties.

After negotiations with Myrtle Beach Farms, Woodside emerged with ownership of sixty-five thousand acres—almost all of Myrtle Beach. He then launched the first stage of development. On the northern end of Myrtle Beach he constructed the Ocean Forest Hotel, a classic high-rise hotel designed to bring big-time glitter to Myrtle Beach. When finally finished, it towered over the strand like a tall, white palace. Guests lodged in luxury. They played shuffleboard on the hotel lawn, splashed in the nearby surf, danced to big-name bands, and dined in chandeliered elegance.

In what is now the Pine Lakes section of Myrtle Beach, Woodside built a twenty-seven hole golf course designed by Robert White, the first president of the Professional Golfers Association. It became known as one of the finest courses in the nation and led to the development of the Grand Strand as a golfer's haven.

But the Ocean Forest Hotel and its golf course were minor creations compared to the project Woodside unveiled in 1929. That year he announced the development of Arcady, a beach resort for the upper class that would be the recreational show-place of America. Prospective investors were given an oversized portfolio designed by a New York artist, revealing Woodside's vision for a modernistic Riviera on the Atlantic. Arcady would be Wood-side's greatest achievement, and 1929 would be his big year.

By the 1920s cottages lined the ocean front at Myrtle Beach and were reached by the sandy lane that would later become Ocean Boulevard. *(Horry County Museum)*

The Ocean Forest Hotel was the centerpiece of John T. Woodside's failed vision of Arcady, a modernistic Riviera on the Grand Strand. *(Horry County Museum)*

Vacationers flocked to Myrtle Beach in swelling numbers in the early twentieth century. *(Horry County Museum)*

Instead, 1929 brought disaster. The stock market crash plunged the nation into the Great Depression, brought ruin to banks and businesses, and destroyed John T. Woodside's vision of Myrtle Beach.

Eventually, most of the property Woodside had bought from Myrtle Beach Farms was returned to the company, which resumed development of the resort in a conservative, progressive manner. Despite his disappointments, however, Woodside had dramatically influenced the development of the area. The Ocean Forest Hotel and golf course won widespread attention for Myrtle Beach, created a strong positive image for the growing resort, and lured large numbers of tourists to the Grand Strand.

182

Although the Grand Strand developed slowly through the Depression and World War II, the tourism industry expanded notably during the prosperous postwar years. Then, in 1954, Hurricane Hazel roared in from the sea and blasted the Grand Strand with devastating winds and seas. When the storm had passed, the strand looked like a bombed city. Beach homes were floating in the surf and marshes. Row upon row of cottages had disappeared, leaving plumbing jutting skyward from the sand. Debris littered the beach, the streets, and the marsh.

Yet from disaster rose development. The Grand Strand had to be rebuilt, and with the renewal came a new era of progress and expansion. The Grand Strand would become a major east coast resort, outpacing the vacation land of Florida in many ways,

Gradually Myrtle Beach grew into one of the most popular vacation resorts on the American East Coast.

(Horry County Museum)

and boasting more golf courses than any other region in the world.

The handful of hearty adventurers who came to the beach behind Black Maria in the early twentieth century would be succeeded by millions of modern vacationers. They would still come from regional cities like Florence, Columbia, Charlotte, but they would also come from New York, Cincinnati, Chicago, and Toronto.

Frank Burroughs did not live to see it. He died in 1897, before his railroad even reached the beach. But Burroughs knew what was coming: "Someday," he had predicted, "this whole strand will be a resort."

ACKNOWLEDGMENTS

No one writes a book alone. I'm grateful to many people who contributed to the original publication of this book and to this expanded revision. Among those who deserve special thanks are: Ed Friedenberg, a friend who published the original version of this book; Ron Pitkin and Larry Stone, who breathed new life into some ageless stories; Beth Rogers, managing editor of *Pee Dee Magazine*; Mort Kunstler, who generously shared his superb artwork; Charles Joyner, author of *Down by the Riverside*; Mary Bull, Paul Fowler, Charmaine Tomczyk, Peggy Bates, and other members of Dr. Lynne Smith's staff at Coastal Carolina University's Kimbel Library; Dr. Edward M. Singleton, Dr. Roy Talbert, Col. Bill Baxley, Dr. Fred Hicks, Lisa Graham, Gwen Turner, Debbie Schmitt, Nadine Godwin, Brenda Cox, Bill Edmonds, David Parker, Catherine Lewis, Annette Reesor, Betty Clay, Mike Pate, Jerry Ausband, Dr. Sally Z. Hare, Janice Sellers, Helen Hood, Audrey Garland, Jim Fitch, Gerdon Tarbox, James and Helen Maynard, Laura Quattlebaum Jordan, Tommy and Kay Swaim, Eugenia Buck Cutts, Willis Duncan, Dennis Todd,

Jim Creel, Sr., Brandy Cox, and the staff of *Pee Dee Magazine.*

I'm also grateful to these institutions: The Horry County Museum, Horry County Memorial Library, the Horry County Historical Society, the Belle W. Baruch Center, Brookgreen Gardens, the Georgetown County Memorial Library, the Georgetown County Historical Society, and The Conway National Bank.

Bob Melton and Charles Lunsford endured mosquitoes and summer heat in treks to remote historical sites in search of "living history." Bill and Margaret Outlaw aided this project. So did Ted and Connie Gragg. Jackie Outlaw made essential changes. Newt Outlaw edited the manuscript, and Jimmy Outlaw shuffled paper repeatedly.

I'm also thankful to Faith, Rachel, Elizabeth, Joni, Penny, Matt, and Skip. As always, my parents, Skip and Elizabeth Gragg, gave me invaluable encouragement. The most important assistance came from my wife, Cindy, who endured my sometimes frantic schedule, tolerated my occasional grouchy moods, helped me retain proper perspective, and constantly reminded me of the relevant truth of Rom. 5:8–9.

SOURCES AND CREDITS

Books and Records

Bass, Robert. *The Green Dragoon, The Lives of Banastre Tarleton and Mary Robinson.* Columbia, S.C.: Sandlapper Press, 1973.

――――. *Swamp Fox, The Life and Campaigns of General Francis Marion.* Lexington, S.C.: Sandlapper Press, 1976.

Bishop, Jim. *FDR's Last Year.* New York: William Morrow & Co., 1974.

Burr, Aaron. *Memoirs of Aaron Burr.* Edited by Matthew L. Davis. New York: n.p., 1836.

Civil War Naval Chronology. Washington, D.C.: U.S. Government Printing Office, 1971.

Coit, Margaret. *Mr. Baruch.* Boston: Houghton Mifflin Co., 1957.

Gragg, Rod. *The Illustrated Confederate Reader.* New York: Harper & Row, 1989.

Gregg, Alexander. *History of the Old Cheraws.* New York: Richardson Co., 1867.

Hilborn, Nat, and Sam Hilborn. *Battleground of Freedom: South Carolina in the Revolution.* Columbia, S.C.: Sandlapper Press, 1970.

Hughson, Shirley Carter. *Carolina Pirates and Colonial Commerce 1670–1740.* Baltimore: Johns Hopkins University Press, 1894.

Joyner, Charles. *Down by the Riverside, A South Carolina Slave Community.* Champaign: University of Illinois Press, 1984.

Lachicotte, Alberta. *Georgetown Rice Plantations.* Columbia, S.C.: State Printing Co., 1955.

Lumpkin, Henry. *From Savannah to Yorktown, The American Revolution in the South.* Columbia: University of South Carolina Press, 1981.

Meriwether, Robert L. *The Expansion of South Carolina, 1729–1765.* Kingsport, Tenn.: n.p., 1940.

Middlekauf, Robert. *The Glorious Cause, The American Revolution.* New York: Oxford University Press, 1982.

Miller, Randall M., and John David Smith, eds. *Dictionary of Afro-American Slavery.* New York: Greenwood Press, 1988.

Milling, Chapman. *Red Carolinians.* Columbia: University of South Carolina Press, 1969.

Morris, Richard C. *Encyclopedia of American History.* New York: Harper & Row, 1965.

Quattlebaum, Paul. *The Land Called Chicora.* Gainesville: University of Florida Press, 1956.

Rankin, Hugh F. *The Pirates of Colonial North Carolina.* Raleigh: North Carolina Department of Cultural Resources, 1979.

Rogers, George C. *The History of Georgetown County, South Carolina.* Columbia: University of South Carolina Press, 1970.

Rogers, James A. *Theodosia and Other Pee Dee Sketches.* Columbia, S.C.: R. L. Bryan Co., 1978.

Official Records of the Union and Confederate Navies in the War of the Rebellion. Washington, D.C.: U.S. Government Printing Office, 1896.

Salley, A. S., Jr. *Delegates to the Continental Congress from South Carolina 1774–1789.* Columbia, S.C.: State Printing Co., 1927.

Simpson, Christopher, Katrina Lawrimore, and James Fitch. *The Lynch Family of Georgetown.* Georgetown, S.C.: Rice Museum, 1978.

South Carolina Archives. "Land Surveys and Plats 1731–1776."

South Carolina Archives. *South Carolina General Assembly Minutes.*

Stick, David. *Graveyard of the Atlantic.* Chapel Hill: University of North Carolina Press, 1952.

Svenson, Peter. *Battlefield.* Boston: Faber and Faber, 1992.

United Daughters of the Confederacy, Arthur Manigault Chapter. *For Love of a Rebel.* Charleston, S.C.: Walker, Evans & Cogswell, 1964.

Walker, C. I. *Rolls and Historical Sketches of the 10th S.C. Volunteers.*

War of the Rebellion, A Compilation of the Official Records of the Union and Confederate Armies. Washington, D.C.: U.S. Government Printing Office, 1880–1901.

Whitney, David. *The American Presidents.* Garden City, N.Y.: Doubleday, 1975.

Woodbury, Lowery. *The Spanish Settlements Within the Present Limits of the U.S. 1513–1561.* New York: n.p., 1901.

Periodicals

Charleston News & Courier
Georgetown Semi-Weekly
Independent Republic Quarterly
Myrtle Beach Sun
Myrtle Beach Sun News
New York Times
Pee Dee Magazine
South Carolina Historical Magazine
South Carolina Historical and Genealogical Magazine

INDEX

Rod Gragg is a journalist and a historian. Among his published works are *Confederate Goliath: The Battle of Fort Fisher*, *The Illustrated Confederate Reader*, *The Old West Quiz & Fact Book*, and *The Civil War Quiz & Fact Book*. His books have been selections of the Book-of-the-Month Club and the History Book Club and have earned the Fletcher Pratt Award from the New York City Civil War Round Table and the Douglas Southall Freeman Award for History from the Sons of Confederate Veterans. He is executive editor of *Pee Dee Magazine* and lives in Conway, South Carolina.